CRM OR DIE

CRM or Die

COURTNEY KEARNEY, CPSM
CHAZ ROSS-MUNRO

Manage Your Client Relationships or Perish

Editor: Jessica Hesse
Editorial Project Management: Karen Rowe, www.KarenRowe.com
Cover Design: Iram Shahzadi, irfa6ster@gmail.com

Printed in the United States

ISBN: 9798985141603 (paperback)
ISBN: 9798985141610 (eBook)

Advanced Praise

"The AEC profession is long overdue in understanding the importance of data. CRM or Die does a wonderful job of focusing on why data is so critical. This is a must-read for any C-Suite professional and could also benefit many in marketing and business development."
Peter Beck ~ *Managing Partner of Beck*

"You know it, I know it - managing and distilling data is an essential element of a firm's success. So why do so many firms not have the processes or systems in place to do it? Likely, it feels daunting, takes too much time, no centralized system, no leadership buy-in, the list goes on. That doesn't have to be! Read this book to know how to assess your CRM strengths and weaknesses to make this a team-driven endeavor that supports your business goals."
Tina Myers ~ *Deputy CEO of SMPS*

"CRMs are one of the most powerful, yet grossly underutilized tools by AEC firms. This book is a strong motivator inspiring the action needed to bring your CRM and data to life, aligning your people and processes to drive performance."
Chad Clinehens ~ *President and CEO of Zweig Group*

"The future of marketing and business development will rely heavily on having a robust CRM program; without it, your firm will be severely handicapped. Courtney Kearney and Chaz Ross-Munro are a rarity in the AEC industry: they truly get *it,* and we should all count ourselves fortunate that they are willing to share their knowledge with the rest of us!" **Scott D. Butcher, FSMPS, CPSM** ~ *Director, Strategic Growth Advisory for Stambaugh Ness*

*To the industry we love and
the dedicated professionals that make it amazing.
This book would not be possible without the mentors, colleagues, and
endless support we have received from so many along our journey.*

Contents

Preface

"I think the two of you need to meet. You would really hit it off!" This is what we were told when we were asked to collaborate on a joint presentation covering the expansive topic of client relationship management (CRM) in the architecture, engineering, and construction (AEC) industry.

We both proceeded cautiously, skeptical of whether the other really was as awesome as we had been told. After a few working sessions, it was clear. We really did work great together. That first presentation led to many more, and now this book.

Meet the Authors

Known for her love of data, Courtney Kearney brings her marketing skills and years of experience to the technical world of databases, processes, and numbers. She is the Founder and Chief Data Officer of CKearney Consulting, a CRM and data management firm focused on supporting the AEC industry. Courtney started in the industry at the age of 14 and spent the following four years interning with a general contractor (GC). After graduating from Texas A&M University, she spent a decade as a marketer before starting her firm in 2016. She is a CRM thought leader, a Certified Professional Service Marketer (CPSM), a contributor to the Society of Marketing Professional Services (SMPS) Marketer publication, and now a published author.

Chaz Ross-Munro has more than 15 years of AEC experience as a marketer and most recently as a Software as a Service (SaaS) Manager responsible for providing comprehensive CRM and proposal automation solutions for AEC firms. She has supported over a hundred CRM implementations. This is Chaz's second book. She first authored *Sink or*

Swim Faster! Making a Splash in Marketing Professional Services, which is a great resource to help onboard new AEC marketers. She is a Certified Professional Service Marketer (CPSM), a contributor to the SMPS *Marketer*, previously held a Certified Foundation (CF APMP) through the Association of Professional Management Professionals (APMP), and was a Certified Scrum Master (CSM).

Our combined experience makes us two of the most qualified experts in the industry to bring you this comprehensive guide outlining all you, the leader of the firm, need to know to be successful with your client relationship management process.

Manage Your Client Relationships or Perish

Titling our book *CRM or Die* might seem extreme to some, but we truly believe that firm leaders must embrace the fact that it is vital to manage client relationships well or the business will cease to exist. When firms adopt that core principle, the process around managing their client relationships is prioritized. To be successful, a CRM process must be created, defined, rolled out, and adopted across the company. Leadership must be committed to holding the staff accountable to this process and, in turn, must be held accountable for using the data being collected.

When firm leaders fail to allocate enough resources and attention to their CRM and data management processes and systems, they are in danger of losing the business. This could sound excessive but remember, businesses do not exist without clients, they are the firm's lifeblood.

Kevin Hebblethwaite, FSMPS, Director of Business Development at Stambaugh Ness, nailed it when he described a firm's risk of demise as "an evaporation-into-irrelevancy rather than sudden death. Most clients who depart don't tell us they're doing so — they quietly disappear. The really painful part is that this situation could be happening to you right now without even realizing it!"

Relationships that go unnurtured are at risk of disappearing. Staying in touch with clients comes naturally to some while others struggle to maintain and grow those connections. These employees will benefit the most from a well-defined client relationship management plan and system. Most importantly their clients will benefit and receive a better experience when engaging with your firm.

Leaders who understand that clients are everything to the business also recognize the importance of data. These leaders make data-driven decisions and create a culture that empowers every employee to make their decisions based on data as well. To do this, there must be an accessible system that centralizes the data and makes it easy for staff members to enter, analyze, and maintain information. Your integrated CRM solution is the perfect place for this, and when optimized, it will keep your business moving forward, ensuring that it will not perish!

> *The most important thing to take away from this book is that*
> *CRM is not about a piece of technology,*
> *it is about people and process.*
> *The technology is there to support*
> *your people and your process.*

Four Parts to Unlocking Your CRM Potential

The first part of this book focuses on why. The first three chapters are dedicated to outlining why you need a well-documented CRM process, why a CRM system or tool is beneficial, why data is the future, and why data-driven decision-making is critical.

The second part centers on preparation and everything you should do prior to seeking a technology solution. Your firm's internal processes need to be in order before you look for external support to make the most of your resources and investment. Part three takes place once a platform has been selected and you are in the best position to successfully implement, utilize, and maintain a CRM process and system.

The final part takes us beyond simply functioning and into a place of thriving, where creative innovations and automations can take you to the next level of performance. Chapter 10 dives into the fun part that few firms get to experience, but we know you will because you will take the time to know your *why*, properly prepare, and implement well, allowing you to fully optimize your process, people, and system! Throughout the book, we will be utilizing real-world case studies (anonymized for privacy) to illustrate practical applications of these principles.

Foreword

"A leader's goal is to make decisions based on facts and figures rather than emotions or opinions. When great leaders harness the power of data, they turn data into information, information into insight, and insight into understanding, which empowers data-driven decisions."

"According to a 2018 FMI report on big data, 95.5% of all data captured goes unused in the engineering and construction (E&C) industry."

Those two statements caught my attention. When efficiency and effectiveness are critical to technical and financial success, what stops firm leaders from using data to improve the ways they serve clients and grow their firms? We use such a small slice of data to drive our strategic direction. What if we gathered, analyzed, and distilled *all* our data — operations, finance, marketing and business development, human resources — to find those paths? What if… all our decisions were made with a focus on delighting our clients, and that led to repeat business, engaged staff, and sustained growth?

A company's success is directly tied to successfully maintaining and growing client relationships. Regardless of your role, your firm's profile, or the markets you serve, a poor client relationship management (CRM) process will cause your firm to flounder. Strong words… but true. Leaders who understand how to harness the power of data and help build a culture of decision-making based on the insights from that data hold the future of the business.

This book shows you how to be that leader. Regardless of where you are in your CRM journey — planning, evaluating solutions, or already implementing, maintaining, or improving a system — I am confident you will find the tips and approaches in these chapters helpful.

Courtney and Chaz offer a fresh perspective on the processes, data, and tools involved in CRM. It's more than technology; it's about your firm's process and people and how they work together to build relationships with those who sustain your firm — your clients!

When executed correctly, CRM increases profitability, improves efficiency, boosts morale, and bolsters productivity with centralized data, accountability, and transparency. Direction, support, and acceptance start at the top of the firm with you. When you define your CRM system as the new source of truth and set the tone for a company-wide culture of data stewardship, it will transform your business.

Viewing data as a valuable asset and renewable resource that must be protected underscores the logic in making every employee accountable for contributing to the process. We roll out data roles for each employee with specific KPIs tied to their annual reviews. We document our CRM process and train employees at all levels to make data-driven decisions. Our collective actions impact the success of our business.

As a long-time member of the AEC industry, I have watched us get enticed by data. We gather it, but then what? We struggle to audit and analyze data, let alone maintain real-time centralized access to it. As a result, it languishes. We fail to learn from it, and we continue to believe that what we think is correct. When we actually look at what data tells us, many of our perceptions are shredded. You may find that harnessing the power of data leads you to change the way your firm is organized and staffed, how it operates, and, more importantly, how it is perceived by your employees, your clients, and your competition.

This book shows you how to gain control of your data and manage it thoughtfully through an integrated CRM solution and, as a result, how to transform your business. Finding your own data utopia requires leadership focus on process clarity followed by a diligent effort from every member of your firm. These authors will change your perspective on data and challenge you to see your clients, projects, employees, and profits differently. After all, firm leaders who understand that information is power and currency will ensure that their firms thrive and not perish.

Combined, Chaz and Courtney have helped hundreds of professional service firms implement, maintain, or improve their CRM processes and systems. When meeting with C-suite leaders, the common thread is, "I do not know what I do not know. You are the expert, so tell me what I do not know." They help leaders navigate this topic and support, empower, and guide them to success. Their approach shows the value of deciding what you want and mapping the process, then determining how to achieve it. This is no different than any wise decision-making effort: start with a well-thought-out plan. Once you begin, make implementation, use, maintenance, and improvement a quality-focused cycle.

I trust these two to continue to lead the industry forward to a bright future full of data and strong client relationships! Listen to what they envision for all businesses and employees.

The future we envision has every AEC employee starting their day logging into an integrated CRM solution, which we define as a firm-wide system that is integrated into the flow of data to capture company, contact, pursuit, and project information to support managing client relationships, internal processes, and asset management.

Once logged in, the employees are greeted with a fully automated company brief showing how they are doing on their goals, what data has changed since they last logged in or last reviewed the data, and the top trends in the company-specific data analytics. Everyone in the firm can read these comprehensive data stories because there is a well-defined process in place that everyone is dedicated to, resulting in a perfect dataset that always stays up to date. The chief data officer has developed a culture of data stewardship, empowering each member to use data to drive their decisions no matter their role in the company. This creates an industry that values data as a renewable asset and uses it proactively for predictive analysis, which positively affects our businesses and each employee.

Picturing this future motivates and inspires me. How does your firm measure up? Are you on course to be aligned with this version of what is to come? Regardless of your answer, you've selected the perfect book to get you in shape and on the right path forward. In fact, why not take the free 10-minute CRM Self-Assessment Quiz at www.CRMorDie.com to see how you score on your client relationship and data management practices? Then retake it after reading the book and see how much your score improves. Better yet, retake the quiz every quarter for the next year to watch your score continue to increase the more you apply the practices being provided. I'm positive the data points will trend up and to the right for more than just your quiz score if you follow the advice outlined in this book!

Both Courtney and Chaz have dedicated a good portion of their careers to improving the management of client relationships. Put their experience to good use and benefit from their lessons learned, their expertise, and their best practices. I assure you that by the time you finish this book, you will view data as one of your company's most valuable assets, and you will insist that your firm prioritize the process and people behind your client relationship management!

Nancy J. Usrey, FSMPS, CPSM
Design Build Strategic Pursuit Director, Associate Vice President for HNTB Corporation
Author of *Insider's Guide to SF254/255 Preparation*
Author of *Insider's Guide to SF330 Preparation*
Fellow, Certified Professional Services Marketer, and a Past President of the Board of Directors for the Society for Marketing Professional Services (SMPS) representing nearly 7000 members and 57 chapters and implementing a vision of business transformed through marketing leadership.

1

Focus on Process and People

"Start where you are. Use what you have.
Do what you can."

— **Arthur Ashe,**
Tennis Player

CHAPTER 1 KEY TAKEAWAYS

1. Client relationship management (CRM) is not about a piece of technology. Rather, it is about process and people.
2. You need a clear, well-defined, and leadership-led CRM process so every employee knows how to successfully manage client relationships.
3. To optimize and protect your business intelligence, you must have a documented process that is supported from the top down and tracks the flow of data through all facets of the business.
4. As the firm leader, you must provide a clear understanding of how data drives the business and how it is being used to drive decision-making.
5. Employees are most successful when a set of well-defined expectations is given, and leadership consistently holds staff accountable to meet them.

6. Data is an asset and should be treated as the valuable company resource it is, building the foundation of the firm's leadership-led data-driven culture.

Most Common Question and Our Surprising Answer

Business owners, firm leaders, and managers love to ask us our opinion on which CRM is the best. Our response always catches people by surprise: Your best CRM is your internal people, processes, and data, because CRM is *not* about a piece of technology.

CRM stands for client relationship management, and strong leaders know CRM permeates every aspect of a business and every employee plays a vital role in the success or failure of CRM. We know you want the answer to be simple and for us to provide you with the name of a technology tool or platform to maximize your CRM, but there is no such thing as an "Easy" button when it comes to client relationship management!

Even so, there *are* great CRM products and support tools available. However, they will only be successful if you create the proper foundation by first focusing on internal processes. Professional service firms are in the business of relationships, and it is vital to nurture the relationships we have built, in addition to gaining new ones. To do this well, every staff member must have three things from the senior leaders of the company.

1. A well-defined CRM process that is easy to follow and is supported from the top down.
2. A clear understanding of how data drives business and how leaders use it in their decision-making.
3. A set of well-defined CRM expectations they are held accountable to on a regular basis.

Most AEC Firms Leave Money on the Table

Scott D. Butcher, FSMPS, CPSM is a highly experienced professional services consultant, marketer, and thought leader in the AEC industry. He is the author of over a dozen books, numerous eBooks, and a contributing author to *Engineering News-Record* (ENR), PSMJ Resources, Inc., and SMPS. He conducted a survey which revealed that the *effective* use of CRM in the AEC industry is limited, although many firms use CRM programs. The results of this survey are detailed in the SMPS Marketing 2022 report.[1]

According to the report, the future of marketing relies heavily on robust CRM systems and processes, as AEC marketers are increasingly embracing business-to-consumer (B2C) approaches to target clients and prospects. We foresee a challenge with this approach, as B2C marketing centers on something most AEC firms are not good at: capturing and managing data.

Historically, our industry has struggled with data. Sure, we update our contact lists once a year for holiday cards and client gifts, and our email lists might be updated monthly or quarterly if there is a company newsletter. But that is not good enough!

According to an ENR article, roughly 40% of AEC firms believe they will be incorporating account-based marketing (ABM) into their practices by 2030. "The future of AEC marketing relies on a blend of traditional and new marketing approaches, driven by the trifecta of client experience (CX), networking, and thought leadership. According to the SMPS research, these will be the most important approaches to marketing and business development (BD) for AEC firms in the coming years. All three of these tactics require data. Lots of data!"[2]

There is often pushback when it comes to data collection. Why? Some say it is because we are all too busy, overworked, and stretched thin, or the cost is too high to have the necessary licenses, or it is too expensive to have billable staff entering data. In some firms, there is a pull between operations and sales, prioritizing the billable side of things. This dynamic can lead to more focus or importance being placed on operational systems and data rather than client relationship management solutions. Leadership needs to resist this behavior, as both are equally important to the success of the business, and firms should not substitute one for the other!

We have encountered all these barriers and more, and although those obstacles might have some validity, they do not get us to the root of why our industry struggles with data. The real problem is that not enough leaders see the value in data, and therefore, there is little to no data stewardship in our industry.

According to Dun & Bradstreet (D&B), data stewardship is the responsibility of ensuring that data policies turn into practice.[3] This is what is missing: Leaders must mandate the creation of data policies and standards, require that they be put in place, and then hold themselves and their employees accountable for being good data stewards.

Data Is an Asset

According to a 2018 FMI report on big data, 95.5% of all data captured goes unused in the engineering and construction (E&C) industry.[4] That percentage is probably a little lower today but is still not where it should be. In fact, a recent poll conducted by ENR shows that 74% of people think their AEC firm does not harness data well.[5] This should be alarming to you as a leader, especially when you stop to consider that data is one of your firm's most valuable assets. Unfortunately, most professional services firms see data collection and management as an expense or a burden rather than an asset and a renewable resource.

In 2006, Clive Humby, a famous British mathematician, coined the phrase "data is the new oil." He explained how data is a valuable resource, particularly when refined, and how it is the driver of growth and change. If data is unrefined, it cannot be used; it must be changed to become a valuable entity to drive profitable activity. Data must be broken down and analyzed for it to have value.[6] Peter Sondergaard with Gartner Research expanded on the concept during a speech in October

2011 when he said, "Information is the oil of the 21st century, and analytics is the combustion engine."[7]

Data is no doubt an important raw material. Unlike other resources, information does not wear out over time. Conversely, the knowledge and insights gained breed more intelligence and understanding. Contrary to other resources, the more you use data, the more data you will have, not the other way around.

When great leaders understand that data is everything, they harness its power by turning data into information, information into insight, and insight into understanding, which empowers data-driven decisions. A leader's goal is to make decisions based on facts and figures rather than emotions or opinions. Chapter 2 goes into this further, as well as the analytics you should review regularly.

In addition to using the data, you want to create a culture of data stewardship. As the leader, you set the tone for how others in the firm value data, from its hygiene and quality to its usage and effectiveness. We cover this in greater detail in Chapter 9, as data maintenance is just one factor in the success of your CRM.

Time to Update the C-Suite Job Description

Some feel the next generation of chief executive officers (CEO) will be former chief data officers (CDOs) or chief information officers (CIOs) due to the impact data has on business. Those who understand how to harness the power of a company's data and help build a culture of decision-making based on the insights from data hold the future of the business.

As data grows exponentially in volume, diversity, complexity, and importance, it raises the question: Should data stewardship be added to C-Suite job descriptions? We believe it should, and in Chapter 2, we make a case for why this position should be at a leadership level and why data management deserves full-time dedication.

Data Culture Comes from the Top

Every role in a company involves data. For data to be used successfully, a culture shift is required, but it *must* happen from the top-down. Prioritizing data, creating data policies, and building accountability into every role will ensure that this valuable company asset is protected and not diminished or lost. In fact, according to a D&B survey, one in five businesses lose revenue and clients due to incomplete data.[8] In addition, SMPS research found a lack of data entry and a lack of upper management driving CRM use were the primary reasons for CRM ineffectiveness. The great news is you have the power to fix both.

> *The most important thing to take away from this book is that*
> *CRM is <u>not</u> about a piece of technology,*
> *it is about people and process.*
> *The technology is there to support*
> *your people and your process.*

Case Study: Leadership Buy-In Is Critical

"Stop right there. I do not want to hear about any project lead or pursuit unless it is already in the CRM system!"

Hearing the CEO of a general contracting firm say this in a meeting was monumental. Here was a leader who truly understood the power of accountability and what it meant to hold employees responsible. This CEO knew that if he let the business developer continue to talk about the lead, it would never make it into the system, and the process would not work. The expectation was for all leads to be entered, and he was willing to implement accountability to ensure it happened. The process had to be followed in order for the CEO to get the data he needed for the board of director meetings so leadership could make data-driven decisions.

If you are a firm leader, you know how much of the business's success depends on you, and the endeavor for CRM is no different. Leadership must demonstrate buy-in and show support for the CRM process, the system, and data management, setting the tone and expectations for others to follow.

If you are not in a leadership position, encourage your leader to read this chapter to understand their role in the firm's success in managing client relationships. In the meantime, we encourage you to start listening to leadership to figure out what data they are missing and what information they need or could use to become better educated in making business decisions.

Starting Small Can Lead to Huge Results

Emmalee was the CRM Manager for a general contracting company, Phillips Lindell Contractors. Each week at the marketing meeting, she listened to Jessica, the CEO, constantly ask which pursuits needed bonds. Jessica was always worried about bonding, spending hours every month updating spreadsheets to determine the current capacity. The insurance company and board of directors also required that this real-time data be presented monthly. Emmalee was surprised the CEO was the one slaving over the numbers and stuck so far in the weeds. She also knew she had the solution, but she was overwhelmed by the thought of getting the entire group on board with entering the necessary information into the CRM system.

She decided to tackle this giant task one step at a time. She began by learning the company's internal processes surrounding bonding. Emmalee met with accounting, BD, and pre-construction to understand the data they captured to gather the necessary information in the CRM system. Her end goal was to provide the CEO with a report that displayed the real-time bonding capacity anytime she needed it.

After collecting all the necessary data, Emmalee prepared the report and gathered the courage to walk into the CEO's office. She pulled up the CRM and logged in. There, on the homepage, sat a link that read "Real Time Bonding Capacity." Jessica's eyes lit up, and she immediately clicked the report link. To her surprise, she recognized the pursuits and current projects, all with real dollars and dates. After what felt like an eternity of silence, she simply responded, "What will I do with all the time I used to spend updating the spreadsheet?"

Emmalee was thrilled, but her internal fear was palpable. How was she going to keep the report up to date? Data accuracy would be critical for Jessica to remain confident in the report and the CRM system. Given how much effort it took to get the report ready, how would Emmalee accomplish that task moving forward?

Emmalee was surprised when the burden of maintenance did not fall on her alone. The following Monday, everyone gathered around the board room table, and instead of kicking off the meeting with the typical round-robin style updates, the CEO pulled up the CRM and pointed to the link on the home page dashboard. Jessica explained how the CRM system was the new source of truth and made it clear that everyone in the room was responsible for entering and keeping all pursuit and project data current and accurate. She went on to explain why she needed the information and how critical it was to the company that her bonding report stay up to date.

Did anything in that quick story resonate with you? What spreadsheet do you spend far too much time on? Who on your staff needs to be held accountable? Who do you need to tell to "stop right there" because you will no longer listen if it is not first captured in your CRM platform? Do you have a clear process that you have told employees they are expected to follow?

Managing Relationships Comes Down to Process

Do you as a leader understand that CRM is not just a tool or platform but a vital part of everyday business and your firm's culture?

Do your employees know what your client management process is and what is expected of them? For instance, when they meet a prospect, what are they expected to do with the contact's information and the information they glean from their encounter? Do they enter the name and email into Outlook and end it there, give the business card to an admin, or scan the card on their phone and enter it into a database? When a new contact has a lead for the firm, where is the opportunity supposed to be captured? Please, do not say an Excel spreadsheet! That said, if you *are* using spreadsheets for client relationship management, do not worry. This is the right book for you to read to learn how to leave Excel behind and get your data into a centralized system to maximize your profits.

To continue probing, once the potential business opportunity is discovered and captured, what qualifies it as a lead worth pursuing, and what makes it valuable enough to spend time and resources on? Is there a formal go/no-go questionnaire, or does an informal discussion take place? If the lead is determined to be a valuable pursuit, who is responsible for maintaining the information and keeping it up to date in the spreadsheet or database? When other department resources like marketing or estimating are needed to help with the pursuit, how are they notified?

Ideally, the prospect becomes a client, and the pursuit is won, but what happens then? Who is made aware of the win, and how? What data is collected at the start of the project? Where is the project information captured, how often is it updated, and who is responsible for gathering the data? Once complete, who maintains the relationship with the client to ensure that you enjoy 100% client retention?

Managing client relationships comes down to process, and your answers to the above questions form your CRM process. We go into further detail on how to develop and hone your CRM process in Chapter 4, but read on to discover how to document your procedures, identify gaps, make improvements, and incorporate your CX into the process.

Right Time, Right Fit

It is always the right time to invest in documenting and honing your internal processes, as well as beginning the journey to be more data-driven.

Realistically, it might not always be the best time to purchase a system or platform. A good deal of work needs to happen to get the firm in the right place to successfully launch a tool. If your firm is not yet ready to implement an integrated CRM solution, it should be a top priority to do the work so you can reap the countless benefits CRM has to offer. To discover the many advantages of implementing and utilizing a CRM platform, check out Chapter 3.

We believe firms that are growth-minded, open to change, data-driven, and have leadership support are ripe to reap the rewards of a well-established CRM. If this describes your company, you will benefit from what we cover in Chapter 5 as we help you prepare for a CRM tool. Preparation is required before you evaluate any platform options and make your selection, as we detail in Chapter 6. After a system is purchased, it is time to implement and see the fruits of the groundwork you laid. Chapter 7 focuses on how to have a successful implementation and the pitfalls to avoid. Once the dust settles and all the processes are in place, it is time to hone utilization, which is covered in Chapter 8.

Our Hope and Future Vision

It is our sincere desire for this book to empower professional service leaders with a clear path forward, regardless of where you currently find yourself on your CRM journey.

When we meet with C-Suite leaders, the common thing we hear is, "I do not know what I do not know. You are the expert, so tell me what I do not know." After you finish reading this book, you will never again wonder, "What do I not know about CRM?"

Combined, we have helped hundreds of professional service firms implement, maintain, or improve their CRM processes and systems. We want to add you and your firm to our list of clients who have navigated this topic, and we are here to support, empower, and lead you to success.

The future we envision has every AEC employee starting their day logging into an integrated CRM solution, which we define as a firm-wide system that is integrated into the flow of data to capture company, contact, pursuit, and project information to support managing client relationships, internal processes, and asset management.

Once logged in, the employees are greeted with a fully automated company brief showing how they are doing on their goals, what data has changed since they last logged in or last reviewed the data, and the top trends in the company-specific data analytics. Everyone in the firm can read these comprehensive data stories because there is a well-defined process in place that everyone is dedicated to, resulting in a perfect dataset that always stays up to date. The chief data officer has developed a culture of data stewardship, empowering each member to use data to drive their decisions no matter their role in the company. This creates an industry that values data as a renewable asset and uses it proactively for predictive analysis, which positively affects our businesses and each employee.

We have dedicated a good portion of our careers to improving the management of client relationships. Put our experience to good use and benefit from our lessons learned, our expertise, and best practices. Let us share our love for data with you. We are confident that by the time you finish this book, you will view data as one of your company's most valuable assets, and you will insist that your firm prioritize the process and people behind your client relationship management!

Call to Action

This is your year; this is your moment! Decide right now that your firm is going to shift to incorporate data into its culture, to select and implement an integrated CRM solution, or populate, scrub, and overhaul the CRM system you have been neglecting or underutilizing. This is the time to hold everyone accountable for being data stewards, not only inputting the data but also maintaining useful data about client interactions, prospects, leads, proposals, and projects. Demand that your firm stop leaving money on the table and start capitalizing on the asset and renewable resource of data.

CHAPTER 1 SELF-ASSESSMENT

- Do you understand the big CRM picture? At its core, CRM is **not** about a piece of technology, it's about process and people.

- Is your current CRM process clear, well-defined, documented, and supported from the top down?

- Have you protected and optimized your business intelligence by documenting your data process to track the flow of data through all facets of the business? Is it supported from the top down?

- Have you explained how data drives your business and how it is being used (or not used) to drive decision-making?

- Have you provided a set of well-defined expectations to your employees, and are they held accountable on a regular basis?

- Do you view data as an asset and believe it should be treated as a valuable company resource? If so, how? If not, why?

- Have you visited our website www.CRMorDie.com to access the additional resources?

2

Data-Driven Decision-Making

"Data is like garbage.
You'd better know what you are going to do with it
before you collect it."

— Anonymous

CHAPTER 2 KEY TAKEAWAYS

1. Your goal as a data-driven leader is to run a business that turns data into information, information into knowledge, knowledge into insight, and insight into competitive advantage.
2. Have a plan and know what you are going to do with data before you collect it.
3. Use data to increase profitability, effectiveness, and efficiency.
4. Be a data champion, viewing data as a lifestyle you commit to and work hard to keep.
5. Take action to create a culture of data stewardship, establish data roles, and invest in a data officer.

When garbage stacks up and is not dealt with properly, it quickly starts to stink. If left unattended, it can start to cause an abundance of issues. Data is similar. When left alone, it is worthless. It reeks, and it only leads to problems.

For being two decades into the 21st century, it is shocking how little the AEC industry capitalizes on the power of data. As mentioned in the previous chapter, 90–95% of all data in our industry is going unused. What a waste of capital and resources![9]

According to a recent poll conducted by ENR, 74% of people think their AEC firm does not harness data well.[10] Where does your firm fall in this statistic? Hopefully in the progressive 26%. However, if you are among the majority of firms that have not yet taken advantage of the data at your fingertips, we hope you will change your perspective by the end of this chapter. Challenge yourself to open your mind to see data in a new light.

Data Collecting Versus Being Data-Driven

Some leaders think they are data-driven because they collect data. However, this is not always the case. There is a difference between gathering data and driving business decisions based on insights attained from data. And frankly, most firms gather data like they do trash. They collect information in bins with no plan to use it once it is accumulated. There is no reason to gather data for data's sake.

Part of the planning process should include where data will be stored, how it will be used, how often it will be used, who will maintain it, and, most importantly, why. An integrated CRM solution is a great place to store data, but firms cannot stop there. In addition to gathering and storing information, we must refine and analyze the data so upper management can use the insights to drive their decision-making. Being data-driven takes effort, planning, process, and accountability.

Data Can Increase Profitability

In Chapter 1, we introduced Phillips Lindell Contractors. It was typical for this firm to track the contract type on their projects, but the information was never used. Moreover, their CEO, Jessica, never looked at the project history or current pursuits by contract type.

When Emmalee was hired as their CRM Manager, she reviewed all the data points coming into the CRM system from the accounting software, with contract type being one of those data points. She discovered that the list the firm was using during the pursuit phase was different than the one accounting was using. She began to ask questions and came to understand that this information was being collected because the contract type was a required field. However, no one had ever noticed that neither dataset was being reviewed.

Emmalee worked with Vaughan, the Marketing Assistant, to review all projects from the last ten years to see what contract type was the most profitable for the firm. They compared the list of profitable contract types to a list of contracts being pursued, which exposed data indicating that most leads had contract types that were not the most profitable. Essentially, this meant the marketing, BD, and pre-construction resources and efforts were being spent chasing less-than-ideal jobs. Once this was discovered, the team shifted their goals and used the contract type field to ensure that at least 70% of all pursuits had profitable contract types. This small change increased revenue by more than 30% in one year!

Did this story hit close to home or ring true for your firm? This is just one example from an endless list of instances where data can bring powerful insights to business. Hopefully it got you thinking about the data your company already gathers that you could be reviewing, analyzing, and using to drive decisions.

Jessica, the CEO, was motivated by this insight and took it a step further. After reviewing more data, she noticed that specific contract types had different project lengths since some required more upfront effort before tapering off. This allowed her to customize workload projections based on the pursuit contract type, which increased staffing decisions. This was terrific because staffing was an area where the company struggled.

This same logic can be applied to all types of data being collected — cost per square foot per market type, profitability by geography, the list is endless. How the information and insights are applied matters more than simply collecting data. Once analyzed and refined, data can be used to decide what markets to devote resources to, what locations to be in, how to utilize staffing projections, and more.

> *The goal of a data-driven leader is to*
> *turn data into information,*
> *information into knowledge, knowledge into insight,*
> *and insight into competitive advantage.*[11]

Increase Effectiveness and Efficiency

Data can help upper management increase their effectiveness and see areas of improvement, as well as gain insight and control.

This can be achieved with data you already collect; you just need a new perspective on how to utilize it. For example, some architecture and engineering firms install software to better monitor how employees work so they can more efficiently charge time based on the client files employees opened.

Separately, some contractors track when materials arrive on a job site, where the supplies are placed, and how often they are moved, reducing the amount of time unused materials are on-site, as well as decreasing the number of times materials are touched/moved until used. This data helps better utilize the job site layout, as well as increase safety and efficiency. The initial investment of resources required to gather this data is worth the powerful outcome of insight, savings, and productivity it provides.

When it comes to the efficiency of the firm's marketing resources, the average time and cost to create a proposal is another dataset that can and should be monitored. Each step of the pursuit can shed light on possible inefficiencies or areas for improvement.

Knowing your company's win rate or hit rate is standard practice, but do you know it by office, profit center, geographic area, client demographic, contract, or project type? The value of collecting *and* analyzing data is the ability to see where the business is losing money or operating inefficiently, providing opportunities for improvement. Leaders armed with knowledge can identify what markets to prioritize, and potentially what markets to leave.

Moreover, marketing is most effective when focused on strategy rather than hunting down the same information time and time again or submitting every bid, *hoping* to win. Likewise, marketers with a successfully integrated CRM solution can enter discussions about strategy and the firm's future, allowing these marketers the opportunity to transform the business.

Data-Loving Marketers

Typically, marketers are willing to adopt initiatives to increase their efficiency and productivity, and the department is usually small and agile enough to make changes quickly. This makes marketing a great place to start testing different data collection methods. For example, they could make a list of pursuit elements — contract and project type, market, geographic location, amount — isolating the important data points, and begin collecting the data on the next few proposals. Have them track the amount of time they spend on the proposal, and feel free to expand to include all staff members involved in the pursuit.

Data can simply be captured and tracked in a spreadsheet, documented by the quarter-hour or according to a general estimate jotted down at the end of the day. The goal is to have the total hours spent on the proposal at the end of the deadline. The last step is to track whether you won or lost the pursuit. Then repeat this for the next couple of proposals and tweak the process, honing the efficiency.

Over time, a data story will emerge. Some proposals take less time, while others take a tremendous amount of time. What is the common factor? If it is not obvious what is driving the difference, dig in to find the root cause.

This daily tracking will be worth the effort when you have hard evidence that suggests what changes could be made and what decisions should be discussed by leadership. For example, the data collected might show that hard bid jobs are not worth chasing because the firm has only won 5% of the hard bid projects pursued the previous year.

Barrier or Champion?

According to research completed for the SMPS Marketing 2022 report, the top barrier for firms successfully using their CRM systems is a lack of data entry from firm principals and seller-doers. The second was upper management not requiring that the CRM be used.[12]

Scott Butcher says client-facing staff are the front line of data collection, as they are receiving data-rich information that is ripe for collection. They have the names, titles, and contact information for all the key people in the organization, far beyond what marketing may have collected in the early stages of a pursuit. They know when people come and when people go, and they are having important conversations with their clients. However, statistics show that client-facing staff often keep these insights to themselves — despite the fact that these are the exact insights required for CX, thought leadership marketing, ABM, and personalized marketing.[13]

Outside the AEC Industry

Looking to leaders outside of the AEC industry, we can quickly see the importance of the role data plays in our lives. For instance, Amazon's predictive algorithms know what we need to order before *we* even know, and they move those items to a warehouse close by since the data shows that having a same-day delivery option increases the rate of customer purchases. Similarly, streaming platforms only give viewers a few seconds to opt out before automatically starting the next episode, and social media platforms play one video right after the other to increase viewer time. Content creators have gathered enough data about human behavior to know what we like and how we will respond, and they allow data to drive their products and programs. We should follow their lead and begin to do the same with the vast amount of data available in our industry.

In response to these examples, we often hear that these kinds of data-driven decisions are not possible for our industry because AEC firms do not have the same volume of information as B2C platforms. We would like to challenge that perspective. We believe AEC firms *do* have large datasets; they just look different. For instance, architecture and engineering firms track hours spent per project for billing, while contractors collect safety numbers, man-hours, material costs, and time spent on the job site.

Data Is Not a Diet

Growing from data scarcity to data abundance requires one thing: a mindset shift. To make this change, we need to understand that data is not a diet. It is a lifestyle.

Most companies collect data simply to prepare a report for a single event or purpose, and once it is over, the data is shelved until the next iteration. Maybe your firm has a quarterly or annual company-wide meeting or a bimonthly marketing and BD meeting to review the number of pursuits, win rates, and goals versus actuals. It is a scramble to get the data into the spreadsheet or system to produce the pie charts, but after those meetings are over, the data is no longer reviewed.

This is similar to how many of us suffer through a 24-hour fast, endure a rigorous juice cleanse, or push extra hard at the gym to get down to a target weight, only to promptly resume our previous lifestyle as soon as the arbitrary goal has been reached. Approaching data as a one-time, start-and-finish project or a quick, rushed assignment for a one-time presentation closes you off to an abundance of valuable insights that could increase your productivity and profitability, much in the same way crash-dieting may be effective in the short-term but carries long-term negative consequences.

People who transform their health understand that success comes from small actions repeated consistently over time. Similarly, data becomes a powerful, positive influence when approached as the foundation of company culture. We often fail when we try to cut out sugar, begin a meditation practice, *and* jog three miles a day all at once. Similarly, we do not often succeed in trying to overhaul company culture all in one day.

One of the keys to breaking the diet cycle and making data a lifestyle is to start small. Have your staff identify the data that should be collected, decide where in the CRM solution it will be stored, set the expectation of how often it should be entered, and agree on how it will be used. We recommend starting with a small dataset, as this will be useful and not overwhelming.

We tend to abandon programs we feel are too hard, are a chore, or do not bring joy, so it is okay if this first step feels too small. It is more important to see a return on investment and realize how easy the process is to stick to, replicate, sustain, and scale. Once the habit is in place and a dataset has been collected, a data story will emerge. Trends or patterns will provide priceless insights into the company's business practices. If the data reveals a problem or an area for improvement, dig in to find the root cause.

Data Storytelling Is the Future

Continuing to look outside of the AEC and professional services industries, one of the things the B2C market is doing well is using data to tell stories. Data storytelling is a method of communicating data analytics, trends, and insights in the form of a narrative or story. It is a proactive way for everyone to receive a unified data message instead of relying on individual employees to find answers and form conclusions on their own.

You might already engage with automated data stories and not know it. One of the most popular is GameChanger, an app that allows millions of parents, family members, and friends to stay up to date with student athletes' games and stats. This program takes millions of games, including 70% of high school championship games and Little League, USA baseball, and USA softball games, and converts game stats into game recaps. How does a company of 50 people keep up with writing so many game recaps? They automate it with Narrative Science's data storytelling tool, Lexio. Those who cannot attend games in-person are able to read a descriptive play-by-play story instead of trying to decipher a stat sheet or scorecard.

In another example, a company that administers standardized testing for public schools was struggling to provide parents with exam results that made sense to them and were customized to individual students. They used Lexio to create informative paragraphs explaining the student's stats. This technology is applied to many other industries, providing endless examples of the power of data storytelling.

For the business world, we can use this same technology to convert datasets into a customized debrief, reporting a company's analytics in narrative form instead of Excel spreadsheets, charts, or a widget on a dashboard. If your firm is not ready for the aid of machine learning and artificial intelligence (AI) to write tailored news briefs, you can have a data leader write them for the company. The goal would be to train more staff members to become data storytellers, empowering everyone in the company to make informed, data-driven decisions to push the company forward.

We recommend shifting from a situation in which only upper management has insight into the business to a place where everyone is well-versed in business analytics, which pulls back the curtain and creates more transparency. In a data utopia, every employee would know what leadership is looking at and basing their decisions on, especially since the employees are the ones providing the data used to create the reports that are telling the data stories!

Get on the Same Page

When a firm begins to rely on their data, whether that is through storytelling, dashboards, or simply reviewing reports, it can expose junk data, misunderstandings, and a lack of data expectations. Junk data is a result of incomplete or inaccurate datasets. For example, using a pipeline report of all open pursuits to make hiring decisions is great only if the opportunities are all there and in the correct stages with realistic expectations of what work the firm will win.

Similarly, if we think back to the CEO's bonding issue from Chapter 1, if half the projects on her report had a zero in the dollar field, that would be an issue. Junk data is easy to catch if someone is looking for it and can be simple to fix if everyone prioritizes the need for accurate data. Solving the issue of data misunderstandings is a little more challenging to fix because it requires more time and usually a point person to dedicate time to dig in and fully understand the data.

We see the most data misunderstandings occur with dashboard widgets. In the context of a CRM system, a widget is a mini report displaying data in a variety of presentation styles, including simple numeric metrics, tables, charts, and graphs. A dashboard is a collection of these widgets providing an overview of the data you care about most, allowing you to quickly check the health of your company.

With the right integrated CRM solution, dashboards should be easy to create, customize, and share. However, it is easy to make assumptions about what is being displayed. We caution you to avoid assuming anything and always dig in to make sure you know exactly what is being displayed on your dashboard.

Take the open pursuit pipeline widget displayed below in Figure 1. The widget must have a clear and descriptive title, so every user knows what exactly is being displayed and how it is being illustrated.

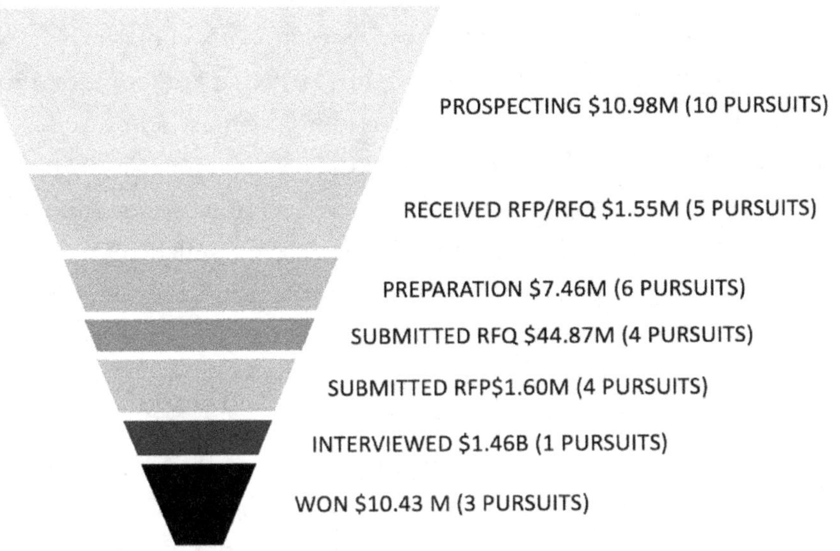

Figure 1. Sample pipeline widget

The following are some things to think about and clarify for users.

- Does the shape of the funnel change based on the dataset, or is it always a funnel regardless of what the numbers show?
- Is each section of the pipeline dynamic or static? If it is responsive, is that based on dollars or quantity?
- Is the widget displaying all data in the system, or have filters been applied to limit the data being displayed?
- If there are multiple dollar values, which dollar amount is being used — estimated fee, project value, factored fee, etc.?

Using the title of the widget to tell users about the data being displayed is important. For example, the title for Figure 1 could be 'Total Estimated Fees for All Open Opps' or if we changed the dollar field and filtered the data the title would be 'Total Project Value for All Open Opps Created This Year.'

If this pipeline widget was on your home page when you logged in to your integrated CRM solution, what would you think? Upon first glance, you might see the shape of the funnel and assume the early stages are the healthiest, funneling down to the wins, and feel confident that the projected pipeline shows everything is in order. However, upon further investigation, you might learn that the cone or funnel shape is static and does not change based on the data.

If you look closely, the biggest section by dollars is at the bottom and not on top, as you might think. In fact, each section of the funnel in the opportunity pipeline is a stage in the project pursuit lifecycle and is a different thickness or height. You might assume the difference is tied to the total dollar amount for the opportunities in each stage. If that were the case, the Interviewed section would be the thickest/tallest with a total of $1.46 billion, but instead, it is the thinnest/shortest. Digging into the data reveals that the dynamic feature for this specific pipeline is connected to the number of opportunities and not the dollar volume.

This small example illustrates the importance of fully understanding your data, how it is displayed, the story it is telling, and how the data impacts the business decisions being made. One of the ways to do this is by explaining what users are seeing with supporting narratives. This could be provided in a separate document or next to a widget on the home page of the integrated CRM solution as seen below. The more communication surrounding your data, the better. It will decrease misunderstandings, reduce the need for assumptions, and lessen the possibility of inaccurate insights being drawn.

The last thing that can come to light is a lack of data expectations, whether that is in the frequency of data entry, what data is needed, the trap of comparison, or having unrealistic goals. Every employee needs to understand how often they should be entering the necessary information, where to enter it, and what fields of data are needed.

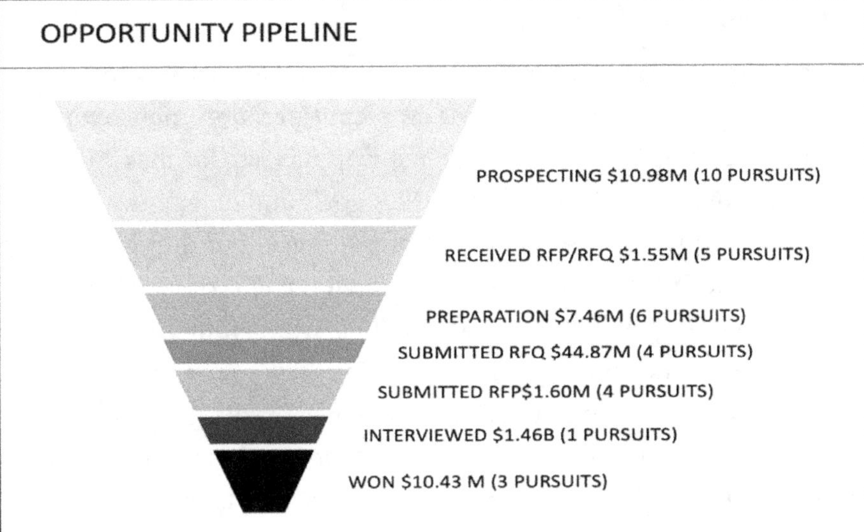

Pipeline Goal: We want to keep the pipeline widget a true funnel with the largest dollars at the top narrowing to the smaller dollar amounts at the bottom. If we have a goal to win $10M, there should be a minimum of $200M in the early pipeline stages. Our data trends show we shortlist 25% of the projects we pursue, we interview for 50% of those, and our win rate is 40%.

Pipeline Dollars: Our early stages are Prospecting, Received RFP/RFQ, Preparation, Submitted RFQ, and Submitted RFP must total more than $200M
The Shortlisted stage must be greater than $50M
The Interviewed stage must be greater than $25M
Wins must be greater than $10M

Calculations: Total Pursuits x 25% = Shortlist Goal x 50% = Interview Goal x 40% = Income Goal
$200M x .25 = $50M x .5 = $25M x .4 = $10M

Current Pipeline: Our early stages total $66.46M which is concerningly LOW! We have zero pursuits in the shortlisted stage; however, we have one $1.46B pursuit in the Interviewed stage with an 85% win probability and we have already won $10.43M this year. This tells us we are in good shape for bookings and need to focus our attention on filling the pipeline with long-lead and early-stage pursuits to fill the $133.54M gap.)

Figure 2. Sample data narrative

The Danger of Comparison

The risk of comparison comes into play when firms are looking at outside standards and not taking into consideration their own metrics first. Looking internally at the makeup of your business provides the insight that should shape your firm's goals and objectives. Industry standards are great to use as a point of reference, but they are not the be-all-end-all and should be viewed through the lens of your own data.

If the industry average hit rate is 40%, while your firm's hit rate is only 25%, do not jump to the conclusion that something is wrong. Rather, take time to consider all factors — the market, geographic location, economic conditions, staff capacity, or longevity. A 25% hit rate is great for staff members new to the team who are pursuing work for a new service line in a new office that recently moved into a developing market. Conversely, the same hit rate is not good for a seasoned team in an established market pursuing work for a well-known service the firm provides.

The Pareto Principle states roughly 80% of our business should come from repeat clients, leaving 20% for new clients.[14] Although this is a good rule of thumb, it might not be right for your business, and therefore, the comparison could be damaging.

According to a PSMJ Benchmark Survey, the size of your staff, the service you provide (A, E, or C), the geographic location, and the market all factor into the percentage of work obtained from previous clients.[15] The survey results showed that firms with 1 to 20 employees averaged 70% repeat business, whereas companies with over 200 had a mean of 81%, while those in the housing market only had 68% from repeat business. Many examples could be shared that demonstrate why comparisons should be made lightly and statistics viewed in the context of your own data.

Non-Punitive Data

For most of the examples we have given, the data has been positive, intentionally. It is important that leadership builds a data culture that encourages employees to be data-driven instead of being punitive.

Key performance indicators (KPIs) are a good gauge for the company's data culture. However, are KPIs only used when trying to build a case to fire someone? Conversely, are KPIs used to praise employees and reward their efforts?

Using data for punitive reasons can cause staff to hide or distort data and potentially pit team members against one another. Data does not have to be punitive! If it is in your firm, act to end that practice today, or every data effort is headed for failure.

For example, if business development is expected to enter all major client interactions and activity into the CRM system, their annual review should include a KPI tied to this expectation.

BD might have a collective goal to bring $200 million in revenue from new clients in a specific market. Their review might indicate the actual new client revenue for the market was $175 million, which shows they only reached 87.5% of that KPI. Quantifiable accountability is helpful for employee measurement but must be relevant. Do not have a KPI tracking the number of user logins. We do not care how many times users log in to the CRM, we are interested in what they do while in the system. A good KPI to track is the conversion rate of contacts. How many contacts did the user convert to a lead, pursuit, or project? The number of opportunities that went through the go/no-go process, or those that the firm was shortlisted on.

Data Stewardship

Once industry leaders recognize data as a significant asset, it is time to create a culture of data stewardship by building a firm-wide atmosphere that supports the use of data. This will empower staff to be driven by the data.

D&B defines data stewardship as the responsibility of ensuring that data policies and standards turn into practice.[7] Simply put, a culture of data stewardship is a firm-wide atmosphere that inspires the use of data and empowers staff to be data-driven.

Data Roles

One of the key pillars of data stewardship is understanding that every employee — yes, *every* single team member — has a data role and takes responsibility for the part they play in the firm's data process. Some may even have multiple roles depending on the task at hand or the duties of their job. These roles are:

- Data editors
- Data auditors
- Data analysts
- Data consumers
- Data leaders
- Data officer

It is important to stress that every person in the company plays a data role and impacts the success of the business. This understanding is part of growing a culture of data stewards. Part of being a good steward is knowing what role each person plays. To have usable, centralized data that can be trusted and validated, every employee must enter information into the necessary systems and follow the documented process to protect the firm's business intelligence.

DATA EDITORS

Every employee is a data editor, someone who enters data into a system and follows a process to maintain the proper flow of information — whether this is the receptionist who keeps the company's phone directory up to date, the business developer who enters the leads, the marketer who tracks pursuit activity, the project manager who updates client and project information, or the CEO who provides intel about their business relationships and new projects. Everyone plays a part in keeping the flow of data moving through the process.

DATA AUDITORS

Auditors are responsible for monitoring information, systems, and processes to ensure functionality and efficiency. For example, you may have an accounting data auditor to run maintenance reports and ensure that all projects have accurate dollars, or a marketing auditor actively ensuring that every contact has an email address, or a business developer auditor making sure every pursuit has dollars and dates populated.

DATA ANALYSTS

Turning data into information and information into knowledge is the responsibility of the data analysts. These team members might also have auditing duties, but not every auditor has the skills to analyze. It is vital that analysts understand the business to accurately convert data into usable knowledge. Senior analysts can go a step further and extract insights from the data and look for trends.

DATA CONSUMERS

Those in leadership and upper management take the work of the data analysts and put it to use, consuming the knowledge and insights to make data-driven decisions. This is how data is turned into competitive advantage! That said, the consumer role does not have to be limited to those in leadership. All team members can become data storytellers, making informed, data-driven decisions that push the company forward.

DATA LEADERS

Policies, standards, and processes must be created, clearly defined, and established for every employee to commit to their data role successfully. The data leaders are the ones who assist with putting these in place, monitoring them, and ensuring that they are enforced and maintained. This group also oversees the information systems and data flow between integrated platforms.

DATA OFFICER

For a culture of data stewardship to be successful and flourish, one's primary role must be to drive the firm's use of data, holding staff accountable to continue to be data-driven and leading the effort to stay focused while also innovating the use of all information. Whether your firm can have a chief data officer (CDO), chief information officer (CIO), chief digital officer, data director, or CRM manager, the important thing is that the role exists and is prioritized. This position must not be an afterthought or taken lightly; it needs to be occupied by someone who understands how to capitalize on the power of the company's data, build a culture of data stewardship, develop data-driven decision-making, and enrich the future of the business.

As data grows exponentially in volume, diversity, complexity, and importance, it raises the significance of this role. Four years prior to this writing, in 2017, Gartner predicted that by 2021, the CDO office would be seen as a mission-critical function comparable to information technology (IT), business operations, human resources (HR), and finance in 75% of large enterprises.[16] Surprisingly, Gartner's 2021 CEO and Senior Business Executive Survey showed that less than half of large companies have a CDO.[17] As pointed out earlier, the role of data officer can have many titles — CDO, CIO, digital officer, data director, etc. — so it is understandable that the survey results do not accurately represent all those filling the role of the data officer. This is confirmed by Gartner's prediction that by 2023, 50% of chief digital officers without a chief data officer (CDO) peer will need to become de facto CDOs to succeed.[18] Regardless of the statistics, CDOs have pivotal roles in accelerating the business and development of a data-driven organization.

All too often, we see companies miss the mark and fail to prioritize this critical role. Do not fall into the trap of thinking that someone on your staff can tack this onto their existing role. We also encourage you not to let the responsibilities be handled by a committee or to just add it to marketing's plate. Data really is a full-time job and needs the attention of someone who can devote the appropriate amount of time to protect, nurture, and grow this limitless company asset.

If you do not have a position for a data leader yet, here are a few reasons why the position is critical to your company's success.

- Data is a living organism that needs to be monitored full-time.
- Firm-wide data stewardship is only successful when policies and standards are created, enforced, and maintained.
- Data integrity is crucial to the success of any database or system.
- Users need ongoing support — training, documentation, processes, etc.
- Communication of changes, direction, expectations, etc., must be consistent and thorough.
- There will be exponential growth and changes to the company's data, systems, and processes, which must be managed well.
- In addition to internal data, there is external data to consider (FMI, Dodge Data & Analytics, CMD Group, etc.).
- It is vital that someone understand the big picture of how leadership wants to use and leverage data to provide direction and proper oversight.

Case Study: A Data Leader Is a Necessity

Checking back in with Phillips Lindell Contractors, we saw earlier how CRM Manager Emmalee was asking probing questions about contract types. Because she was solely focused on the client relationship data, she was able to ask leadership what they wanted entered into the system as an opportunity or pursuit. Should every fee proposal, bid letter, or statement of qualification (SOQ) be input? What about indefinite delivery, indefinite quantity (IDIQ), change orders, or on-call contracts? No one had ever been able to achieve this level of specificity before due to competing priorities.

After facilitating discussions with leadership, it was obvious that everyone had their own opinion, and no policy or standard was in place. Some were only entering the fee proposals they won and others only when they heard back from the client, while one office did not enter them at all. This resulted in a skewed hit rate and inaccurate revenue projections, and no one ever knew!

It took Emmalee being in a dedicated role focused on getting to the root of what data was being entered and reported. If she had not been in this position, the question would not have been raised, and decisions would have been made on false information and incorrect insights.

In addition to these potential benefits, there is the technology component to the role. The individual needs to fully understand the integrated CRM system and any other technology platforms it is connected to, as well as the big picture of data as information flows throughout the business.

In today's world, technology changes quickly, a trend which we anticipate will continue and even accelerate. Therefore, it is important that someone stays on top of the software the firm has in place to ensure optimization. If someone does not stay knowledgeable and continue to communicate the database changes or new features as well as the direction the company is going with the system, the platform and all processes will fail, and with it, any momentum and buy-in will quickly dissipate.

If a company is willing to spend the upfront cost to purchase a piece of technology as well as the time, money, and effort needed to implement it, leadership needs to be prepared to preserve that investment. A CRM system should be viewed as a similar investment to that of new software or IT equipment, and the company should plan to support the investment over the long term with the proper maintenance, upgrades, troubleshooting, etc.

Commit and Act

Once you realize how influential data can be, it is time to commit and act. Those who maintain a healthy lifestyle know the importance of action. There is no *perfect* time to begin, but the *best* time is now!

We encourage you not to wait for ideal circumstances, as those will never arise. Instead, take a few moments right now to clarify your goal, put your commitment in writing, share it with a fellow principal or colleague, and then make the commitment public, communicating it company-wide. Stay focused on progress over perfection, and you will uncover the value of the compound effect for success.

We are excited about the business insights you will gain from the data collected in the integrated CRM solution, information you will analyze and turn into knowledge, understanding, and competitive advantage that will empower your new data-driven decision-making process.

Remember, social media platforms were able to perfect their algorithms because they decided to see touchpoints, typing speed, likes, and shares as data. They committed to collecting information, analyzing it, and implementing the results. These companies did not see data as a one-time project. Instead, the importance of data has been deeply ingrained in their company culture and individual daily habits.

In the same way, we are confident that data can become a powerful influence in the AEC industry. It is time to build a healthy lifestyle for the long term. Let us ditch the diets once and for all and commit to becoming data-driven!

Data Utopia

Now that you understand how to be a data-driven firm, how would you describe your data utopia? Do you envision one unified dataset that flows through all business systems? Do you wish that contact information would seamlessly flow from Outlook and mobile devices to the CRM system, that pursuits would push to accounting and other project management tools upon winning new projects, or that the CRM would pull the accounting data back over for complete asset management? In your utopia, is all double data entry eradicated and all data inefficiencies eliminated?

In our utopia, every AEC employee starts their day by logging into their integrated CRM solution, where a fully automated company brief is waiting for them, along with a customized list of objectives. Everyone in the firm can read this comprehensive data story because there is a well-defined process in place that everyone is dedicated to, resulting in a perfect dataset that always stays up to date. The chief data officer has developed an impeccable culture of data stewardship, empowering each member to use data to drive their decisions, no matter their role in the company. This creates an industry that values data as a renewable resource and an asset, views data as a lifestyle and not a one-time crash diet, uses data to be predictive and therefore reduces reactive behavior, and of course, always uses data positively, never punitively.

Will you help us bring our data utopia to life?

CHAPTER 2 SELF-ASSESSMENT

- Are you a data-driven leader? If so, what can you do to improve the use of data at your firm? If not, what is holding you back?

- Does your firm have a clear data process to turn data into information, information into knowledge, knowledge into insight, and insight into competitive advantage?

- Are you using data to increase your firm's profitability, effectiveness, and efficiency?

- Are you a data champion committed to view data as a lifestyle?

- Does your firm have a culture of data stewardship, established data roles, and a data officer?

- Have you visited our website www.CRMorDie.com to access the additional resources?

3

Benefits of an Integrated CRM Solution

CHAPTER 3 KEY TAKEAWAYS

1. An integrated CRM solution is a tool to help your firm manage your client relationships and aid in the efforts to win more work. It is **not** the focus; it exists to support the CRM process, your staff, and the business.
2. A CRM platform can increase profitability and create heightened efficiency.
3. A CRM tool can improve morale and increase productivity with centralized data.
4. An integrated CRM solution is a great tool for accountability and transparency.

Case Study: Protecting Important Assets

Brendan, the owner of Brueggemann Civil Engineering, has owned his business for nearly 40 years. After his business survived the Great Recession, he vowed to put in a few more years before retiring. Brendan planned to leave the business to his eldest son Patrick, who has been with the firm for the past 15 years, but the COVID-19 pandemic changed his plans. Now, Brendan is uncertain if he will ever be able to retire because he does not want to leave the business in a weak economy.

Far too many businesses survive one economic disaster only to face another industry crisis right behind it. Many AEC professionals are used to the peaks and valleys, but in the last few years, the hits seem to be coming in more rapid succession. We cannot control external economic factors or industry shocks, but one thing we can control is taking care of the assets we possess within our organizations.

As mentioned in Chapter 1, data is the oil of the 21st century, and unlike other resources, data does not depreciate but instead grows exponentially. The more you use data, the more data you have, not the other way around. The relationships we have within the industry are some of our most important data assets, and they need protection. Many firm owners and industry veterans have done an excellent job of managing these relationships over the years. However, when these leaders and senior staff leave, so do the relationships and the associated potential revenue. But it does not have to be that way!

Protecting the firm's business intelligence, including the relationships and intel that accompanies them, is an important part of the client relationship management process and system. It is a valuable benefit of having an integrated CRM solution but is not the only advantage CRM brings to a firm. In this chapter, we will talk more about the four main benefits of using CRM.

The four main benefits of CRM are to increase profitability, bolster productivity, improve efficiency, and boost morale through the use of centralized data, accountability, and transparency.

Increase Profitability

Referring back to Brendan, he decided to include his son Patrick in his quarterly review of all current projects. As many owners do, Brendan takes pride in the relationships he has created with each of his clients and feels passionately about each project. To prepare for the quarterly review with his father, Patrick pulled together the data for the current projects and reviewed each client's revenue over the past five years.

Patrick is driven by data, so when he began working for the company, he took the small marketing budget and invested in a CRM system. He has been diligently entering data on the company's key accounts, including the clients his father is close with. He has tracked the projects they have pursued with each client, noting those they won and lost — including the reason for the loss — and how much referral work the client brought them, if any.

As the meeting progressed, Patrick became unsettled by how differently he and his father viewed the key accounts. The tipping point was when Brendan brought up long-time client High Wood Real Estate Development Company, saying, "I have worked with them for 15 years, and they are one of our most profitable clients. We have done more than 12 projects with Clint and his team. Going forward, I would really like to see you continue to invest in them. I know they will take care of you in return."

Patrick took a deep breath; he knew what he was about to share would be hard for his father to hear. "Well, Dad, I have been reviewing this account as well as the other 12 projects we have done for Clint, and only five of them have been profitable. Clint always makes a ton of changes, and this really impacts our ability to make a profit on the job. Also, in the past five years, he has not referred a single client, and every reference request we have ever sent has gone unanswered. Honestly, I do not know if this is a client we should continue to invest in as much going forward."

Sometimes, the clients *we think* are the most profitable are not. Profitable clients are not just the clients that pay us on time. Profitable clients should not cost the firm extra resources. Ideal clients are, of course, profitable, but they also refer work to the company and see you as a partner. A CRM solution integrated with the accounting system is a great tool for looking at business relationships holistically to determine if the relationships are beneficial. Unfortunately, as is the case with Brendan, sometimes the relationships we feel are the strongest are, in fact, costing us revenue and resources. An unbiased look at the data might show that some of our favorite clients are not ideal.

Looking at client data instead of relying on gut instincts is a shift that growing firms must make. In the past, looking at a company's growth based simply on revenue was a good indicator of how well a firm was doing. However, if you want sustainable growth within your organization, start to look at your clients *and* their behaviors. Track how much work they refer to you and how they treat the staff during a project, focusing on more than just project history.

Holistic data allows you to make better decisions about which clients to prioritize, which to pursue, and which to fire. In some cases, these decisions are by no means easy, but they are critical to the firm's success. Shifting how you think about clients and only pursuing work with those that are ideal for your firm will allow the firm to thrive and be more profitable, and it all starts with drilling into your client data.

Bolster Productivity

Brendan and Patrick reviewed all active clients and determined which clients were ideal based on holistic data, looking at more than just who was the most profitable over the past five years. Both were surprised that a few of the clients they thought would be at the top of the list were not actually ideal clients. Now, it was time to make changes in how they prioritized the work that came in the door based on the client analysis they had completed. This new awareness changed how they managed the business.

For example, Brendan thought one of his senior engineers, Jacob, was an average engineer because he did not stand out internally. However, after doing the client review with Patrick, they realized Jacob was managing more clients than any of his colleagues. Plus, he received the fewest client complaints. Jacob stayed busy and always seemed to find the next project, consistently bringing work in the door, but he never advertised it. Patrick knew that for the past several years, Jacob had taken it upon himself to hand-deliver the holiday gift to each of his clients, and for the clients he had strong personal relationships with he delivered birthday gifts too!

Because Brendan and Patrick had never done this type of detailed analysis by client — previously, it was by project and at a high level — they could never see the bigger picture to realize what a great job Jacob was doing at managing his client relationships. Brendan felt guilty about the times he had prioritized resources for other engineers who complained about how much work they had when Jacob's workload was close to twice theirs. He also admitted to Patrick that he wished they had taken the time to make this shift years ago.

After completing the new client-focused analysis and making the discovery about Jacob, Brendan told Patrick, "I am thinking we should shift resources around. I previously thought Zach needed more support but based on the types of clients they have and their workload, I can see we should give Jacob more resources instead."

Patrick replied, "I completely agree with you! Zach talks a good game about how busy he is and how he is always strapped for time. He tells us he needs more support, but maybe the root of the issue is that he does not know how to manage his clients as well as Jacob does. It would probably be a good idea to put Zach on one of Jacob's projects so

Jacob can mentor him. This would also provide Jacob with additional support."

Improve Efficiency

These are the kinds of valuable insights a firm can benefit from when using a CRM to manage client data. By utilizing a CRM process and analyzing the data, instead of trying to make an educated guess about which direction to go, the answers become clear. This brings us to the second benefit of using a CRM: increased efficiency. Access to centralized data and resources allows employees to do their jobs better. Leadership having data available to support decision-making increases their effectiveness in addition to their efficiency.

We recognize that collecting data, analyzing it, and turning it into insight is only part of the process; the hardest part of improving efficiency is change management and successfully changing people's behavior.

The decision to invest in data can sometimes be met with resistance, especially when it comes to client relationships. There are often strong feelings involved when discussing the relationships that upper management and senior leaders have spent years cultivating. Some might be concerned about taking billable time to populate a CRM system or feel anxious about changes that will be made based on the data analytics. Meanwhile, others might be nervous that the data will be used punitively or fear that clients will turn their backs on the firm when they realize things are being reprioritized. These concerns are valid and best to face head-on with transparent communication.

It is easier to prioritize resources, make key decisions, and improve efficiency when a firm is focused on using data to determine who their ideal clients are and how to best allocate the appropriate resources to them. Ideal clients come in all shapes and sizes. Professional service firm leaders should focus on having a diverse client base; what that means is different for each business.

The COVID-19 pandemic demonstrated how critical market diversity is to a firm's long-term success. The various markets a firm is in should be driven by data and a strategy that supports the markets you are best suited for, whether it is because they are the most profitable, because they support growth, or due to other reasons. The important thing is that the analytics are regularly reviewed to show the markets you are in remain the best fit. The same is true for diversifying the project sizes, client types (private and public), contract types, and other factors that are specific to your firm.

The bottom line is, once firm leadership looks at the data, it should be unacceptable to go back to old habits and old ways of doing business. When there is a clear path forward that will increase profitability and efficiency, the best thing to do is push forward!

Boost Morale

Using their CRM and detailed analysis, Brendan and Patrick turned data into information, information into knowledge, knowledge into insight, and insight into competitive advantage. They increased profitability by shifting their focus to client-centered data. They started making decisions that improved their internal efficiency while ensuring they still delivered the best service to their key clients. A few weeks after the staffing changes were made that gave Jacob more resources, Brendan was pleasantly surprised when Jacob came to his office.

Jacob was uncharacteristically grinning from ear to ear and enthusiastically announced, "I know I do not usually stop by unannounced, but I just got off the phone with George from Hilton Development. He called to discuss the change in our performance the last few weeks. He has been so impressed with our work that he decided to give us their next three projects. He was going to bid them out but decided not to and will just award them to us. Thank you for the extra resources; it allowed me to be more responsive and make changes quickly, which really sped up the progress. I am able to serve our clients even better than before, and it is paying off!" And with that, Jacob bounced out of the chair and went back to work.

Brendan sat back in his chair, stunned at what had just happened. Because of the CRM data and the insights gained, they were able to recognize their best performer and make changes to get him much-needed resources, which resulted in happier clients and more work! In fact, Brendan realized Jacob's entire department had been in high spirits the last few weeks, including the two newer CADD (Computer-Aided Design and Drafting) techs that were moved over to provide additional support. They seemed to have found a good flow, working well together, and, by the sounds of things, the clients were noticing.

Once a firm prioritizes ideal and profitable clients and allocates resources more efficiently, it is natural to see a pop in performance and morale. When your team is not struggling to win over clients that will never be satisfied, and they are not worried about whether the client's actions are going to negatively impact the project profitability, it alleviates stress and makes their jobs easier. By using a data-driven approach to your client relationships and only focusing on the clients that treat you well, the byproduct is a team with higher morale and the energy to take on more projects and execute them at a higher level.

Protect Business Intelligence

A couple of days after Jacob's announcement, Brendan wanted to go check in to see how the team was doing and if the new projects were coming to fruition. Brendan became self-conscious that he was not remembering the conversation correctly and began to question whether Jacob really had mentioned new projects.

Brendan's memory had always been pretty good, but he had found that after creeping past the age of 70, details were starting to slip more often than he cared to admit. In the past, he would not have hesitated to walk over to Jacob's desk and ask him the names of those projects, but now he feared that if he was wrong, his age would show. So instead, Brendan decided to finally jump into the CRM system his son had been talking about all the time — right after a quick call to Patrick, because he seemed to have misplaced the email with his username and password.

"Alright, you are in," Patrick said as he pulled away from his dad's laptop. "Do you want me to show you around a bit?" Brendan nodded.

Patrick began to walk him through each module of the CRM: companies, contacts, opportunities, activities, and projects. He noticed how each piece of data related to others in the system, and all the information could be quickly accessed through the search bar. He sat back to take a moment to reflect on how things were when he first started the business almost 40 years ago, remembering how he used to rely solely on the Rolodex that sat on his desk and the memory of his office manager to relay pertinent information back to him when working on a request for proposal (RFP). It was always amazing to him how she organized all the information and was able to quickly find exactly what he needed. Now, all these years later, someone had figured out how to take that skill and build it into a CRM. Although Brendan would rather go to a person, he was starting to see how having a system with all this data organized was helpful.

"Wow! It looks like Jacob was not exaggerating," Patrick said, snapping Brendan back to the present. He tried to quickly zero in on what Patrick was talking about. "See here, he created three opportunities in the last week for Hilton Development — with fees ranging between $1 million and $2 million. Not bad!"

As Brendan clicked on one of the opportunities and started reading the description, something about the location of the site seemed familiar to him. "I swear we did work on this site about four years ago. We were working with a different developer; we did a ton of planning for mixed-use development, but it never went anywhere."

Patrick went to the search bar and typed in the name of the developer, and the project popped up: *TGH Development Cypress Hill Project.* "That was it, that was the project!" Brendan exclaimed.

By clicking on the project record, he instantly had access to the contacts he had worked with on the project, fees charged, key dates, and a description of the scope of work. He also saw a Documents section, so he clicked on that and found the Phase I assessment they had completed for the project. Within minutes, Brendan had confirmed he remembered correctly, located Jacob's opportunities, and found project data from four years ago — and he was amazed.

Patrick could see the smile on his father's face and took the opportunity to interject, "Now you see what I have been doing with all the project details you tell me."

Brendan glanced back at his son, replying, "I sure can. This is really helpful. I wish I had gotten on board sooner! I have wasted so much time looking through files and asking people where stuff is when it was likely in the CRM all along."

Centralize Data

A centralized database is a huge benefit of an integrated CRM solution. When marketers, business developers, principals, and project managers begin tracking the amount of time they spend looking for information, it can quickly add up, considering that each person could easily spend 15 to 30 minutes each instance. Adding up that time over the course of a year, it is easy to see how tens of thousands of dollars are wasted due to the lack of access to centralized information.

Another issue that comes into play when firms do not have a centralized database is the correction of information. How many times do employees make the same mark-ups in marketing materials, email blasts, or RFPs? How often does the size of a project change in one submittal from what was listed on the project sheet, a resume, or a mention in the project safety narrative?

Lack of access to a centralized database creates duplicate effort because different people within an organization store files in separate locations. These disparate data sources lead to inconsistencies because there is no single source of truth. A centralized database creates consistency and provides a reliable source of truth, resulting in time savings for its users.

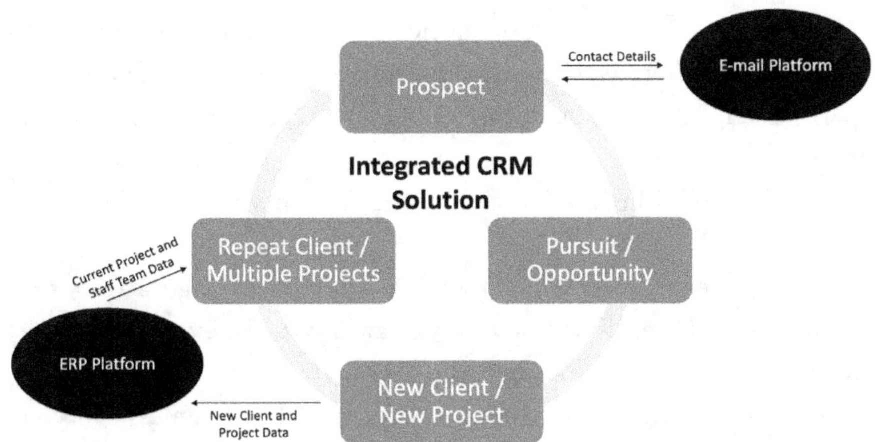

Figure 3. An integrated CRM solution ensures that key information is incorporated during the entire client lifecycle so your firm can better serve the client and leverage that same data to win future projects.

Clear Expectations

Brendan was extremely pleased to see how the CRM was benefitting his organization. It provided clarity on Jacob's pursuit and allowed him to see the full opportunity pipeline, and he found himself going back to the system regularly to look up more and more information.

One thing he was curious about was the performance of one of the junior engineers, Zach. He was always the first person to jump in during meetings and talk about how busy he was and how he had more projects about to land from various clients. At the previous staff meeting, Brendan had told everyone that he and Patrick expected them to be entering all pursuits into the CRM and that they were both using it and monitoring it regularly. In fact, he told the staff that if a project was not in the CRM, it did not exist and would not be taken into consideration.

Two weeks after that meeting, Brendan wanted to see how many team members were regularly logging activities. It was no surprise to him that Jacob had over ten opportunities listed in the CRM with estimated start dates populated and stacked tightly over the next few months. It was possible that they would need to hire a few more engineers if those came through. Brendan started looking at the other team members and came to Zach.

"Hmm... Only two opportunities? That cannot be right," he thought. Well, there was one way to find out what was going on.

"Hi, Zach, how are you doing?" Brendan asked as he entered Zack's office.

Zach seemed a little surprised by the sudden visit. "Fine, how are you doing, sir?"

Brendan began, "Do you remember a few weeks ago at our staff meeting when I mentioned how important it was for everyone to start entering their opportunities into the CRM? It is important that we get better at forecasting our pipeline, and that is hard to do unless everyone is committed to inputting their data. I saw that you only had two opportunities listed, and they are small projects. Is that accurate? I thought at that same meeting you said that Robert at Blanca Partners had some huge work coming your way."

"They do," Zach quipped, "but I do not have time to go into the CRM and type all that information. That is what the staff meetings are for, so we do not have to waste billable time doing data entry."

"No, Zach. Actually, the meetings are when we review the data for insights so we can make strategic decisions that increase our efficiency and profitability. That is what drives our competitive advantage. We have processes and systems in place to protect our business intelligence, like our pursuits and pipeline, but the meetings are not the time for that. And entering this data is not a waste of billable time at all. When I told the staff that if a project was not in the CRM, it did not exist, I meant it. I am here to hold you accountable for doing what is expected."

Accountability and Transparency

The speed of doing business is always increasing, and our decision-making must keep pace. It is easy for leaders to get absorbed in day-to-day tasks and keep moving from meeting to meeting, forgetting to communicate their expectations or the important decisions being made. However, it is vital that you, as the leader, prioritize communication to set the stage for accountability.

When a CRM is utilized effectively, two of its biggest benefits are improved accountability and increased transparency. There are many AEC firms that have operated for years without having a solid grasp on what their opportunity pipeline looks like. Dips in project workload can be discovered earlier if a CRM is utilized, and this can help firms create strategies to overcome peaks and valleys in project flow. It all starts with each team member being honest about the pursuits they are chasing and committing to entering all their information into the CRM — and leadership holding them accountable for delivering on that commitment. Although the AEC industry deals with economic waves regularly, having a CRM with a solid forecast that a firm can trust could mean the difference between reallocating resources and layoffs. If everyone is looking at the same data, the same insights drawn from transparency are available to be enjoyed by all.

The case study of Brueggemann Civil Engineering highlighted the benefits of a CRM tool. Brendan and Patrick were able to identify previously unknown trends that changed their resource allocation, as well as their profit margin. Two great achievements! This case study also showcased the importance of leadership buy-in and accountability. Although Brendan did not initially understand the value of using a new piece of technology, once he saw the true power of data, he recognized the importance of communicating a clear process and establishing expectations from the top-down. Ultimately, everyone at the firm benefitted from understanding that CRM is more than a tool; it is client relationship management in action!

CHAPTER 3 SELF-ASSESSMENT

- Do you have an integrated CRM solution for managing client relationships to help the firm win more work?

- Do you have an integrated CRM solution to increase profitability and create heightened efficiency?

- Do you have an integrated CRM solution to improve morale and increase production with centralized data?

- Do you have an integrated CRM solution to use for accountability and transparency?

- Have you visited our website www.CRMorDie.com to access the additional resources?

4

Business Processes

"If I had an hour to solve a problem,
I'd spend 55 minutes thinking about the problem and
five minutes thinking about solutions."

— **Albert Einstein,**
Theoretical Physicist

CHAPTER 4 KEY TAKEAWAYS

1. Process mapping is the first step in preparing for an integrated CRM solution.
2. Focus 90% of your effort on planning and 10% on the result.
3. Learn the five steps of process documentation: map, identify, review, improve, and monitor.
4. Flip the perspective and create a CX map detailing the journey that your clients experience when working with your firm.

We think Einstein was right. We believe 90% of effort should be spent on planning and preparing for an integrated CRM solution, leaving 10% for implementation and maintenance.

So many firms get this wrong, and this is the number one reason we see CRM systems fail. It is not the software that fails a firm but a firm's lack of internal focus that causes client relationship management to fail. However, we are here to correct this and ensure that your CRM succeeds.

The next three chapters are dedicated to the first 90%. We will spend time digging into processes, wants, needs, and desires, and really clarify the root of the problem that has you positioned to need a CRM. To find the right CRM, you must first understand what the actual problem is before you can solve it with a process or tool.

> *The integrated CRM solution that is right for your firm cannot be identified until you first investigate, document, and refine your business processes.*

Case Study: Importance of Identifying the Root Issue

Aydan, a Marketing Coordinator for Safron Architects, a 100-person architectural firm, was called into a monthly leadership meeting and asked how often the company connects with its tier-one clients. She did not have an answer, and that was a problem.

Her first reaction was to go to accounting and get the list of top clients by revenue for that year and then cross-reference that list with the marketing, BD, and operations departments to see when they last talked to each client. Carrying this out would have allowed Aydan to answer leadership's question, but the real request would not have been met; the process would be onerous to duplicate if they ever asked that same question again, and the underlying problems go unaddressed! This is exactly what Einstein was getting at when he said to focus on getting to the root of the issue instead of spending most of our time on the result.

Instead of leaving the meeting and immediately seeking an answer to the aforementioned question, Aydan stayed and asked clarifying questions. She investigated internal procedures, documented processes, and reported back her findings. This allowed her to identify that what leadership really wanted was an ongoing real-time report that was easily accessible to them and would support their decision-making. When Aydan stopped to ask leadership what they really wanted, how often they wanted it, and how they defined tier-one clients, she discovered so much more than if she had simply accepted the request, made her own assumptions, and produced a one-time list.

Once Aydan took the time to dig in, she discovered that the real request was for data to be continuously captured, maintained, and reported. This would require effort from more than just her, it required the support of leadership to bring attention to what was being requested. She also needed leadership to communicate the changes that needed to be made in order to facilitate their request and explain to other involved employees why these changes needed to happen.

Over time, Aydan identified the data she needed: client revenue earned over time, each client's future potential revenue available for the firm to win, who internally was connecting with the clients, and how and when those actions were taking place. She spent the next several weeks meeting with each department that had the data she needed, investigating the internal procedures so she could outline and document the flow of information.

Aydan learned that accounting captured revenue and actual dollars earned from each client but did not gather potential dollars. The business developers had that information in an Excel spreadsheet, but the data was siloed because BD broke clients down by market. As for who was connecting with clients, how, and when, that was more complex. It involved almost every department — marketing, BD, operations, leadership, technical staff, and even the receptionist. The result was a flow chart documenting the disjointed movement of data throughout the company.

Having the internal process on paper was eye-opening! It revealed double-data entry, information going uncaptured, and decisions being made based on inaccurate or incomplete knowledge. Ultimately, leadership was able to recognize the misuse of a company asset: data.

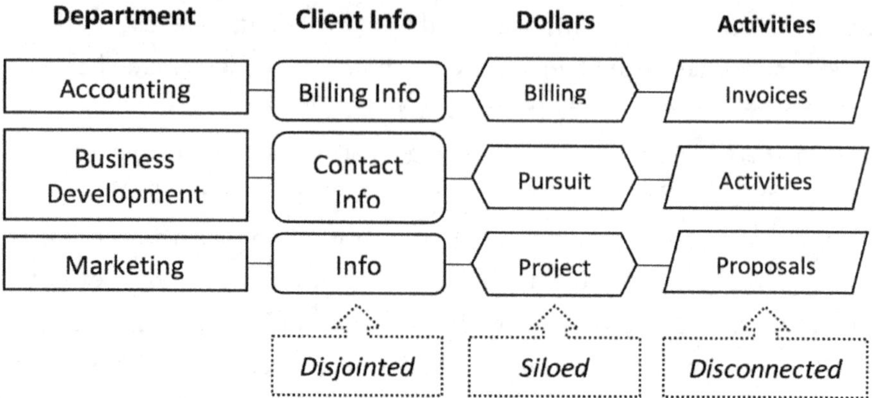

Figure 4. Sample flow chart

After identifying gaps in the process, Aydan was able to present a better process, which leadership reviewed and approved. A marketing campaign was developed to explain the new flow of data and all the steps necessary to make the change successful. At the root of all communication was the explanation of why this change was needed *now*, and how they would sustain the new process for the long term.

Six months after the initial launch, leadership called Aydan into another meeting to commend her for a job well done and to publicly acknowledge her positive impact on the firm. They also took this opportunity to discuss future improvements and expansions to the process.

Lessons Learned

There are several things we can learn from Aydan's experience.

- **Investigate.** Employees should always dig to get to the root of a request, asking clarifying questions and exploring internal procedures.
- **Document.** Getting the process on paper allows everyone to see what is really going on. This should involve more than just a single person or department — break down those silos.

- **Support.** For leadership to receive the requested information changes were necessary, which required top-down support.
- **Responsibility.** Identifying the data needed to complete a request is important, but for ongoing success, the data must be continually captured. This requires a clear process with assigned responsibility.
- **Improvement.** Having the process documented allowed the team an opportunity to see gaps in the process and make changes and enhancements.
- **Communication.** An explanation was sent to the staff showing the new flow of data with a clear set of action items and expectations, along with an explanation of why the change was needed.
- **Clarifications.** Never assume everyone is on the same page. In fact, always assume everyone has a different understanding until clarification is given. Take the time to spell out what you mean and explain/share the reason behind it.
- **Acknowledgment.** The effort to improve things and positively impact the firm was publicly recognized, which reinforces leadership's buy-in and support.

Five Steps of Process Documentation

This story outlines the process we recommend taking when firms start the journey to document and improve any internal process.

1. Map your current internal process.
2. Identify gaps in that process.
3. Review the process.
4. Improve the process.
5. Monitor the process.

MAP THE PROCESS

The act of mapping your process and getting it on paper is the most important step, because it allows you to see problems and areas for improvement. This does not have to be a fancy 11x17 Lucidchart diagram with color-coded shapes that each have a specific meaning. Although those are great internal resources to build, you can just as effectively sketch your process on the back of a napkin.

Wherever you fall on the spectrum, the task is simply to get it down on paper. It does not have to be pretty; you just have to capture it.

IDENTIFY GAPS

Once the current process is documented, the root cause of some of the problems might become clear. Some challenges will have easy fixes, while others might require more digging.

It is important to get to the root of the issue so you can find the correct solution. Looking for gaps in the process means taking the time to see where things bottleneck, where data is lost, or where misunderstandings are happening. Is data being entered twice — or even more times — into several different places or systems? Does one department have information that another one needs? Is a deadline or reminder frequently being forgotten or missed? Is there a lack of transparency, or is there decentralization that is causing frustration? Is leadership getting inaccurate or incomplete information because something is missing in the flow of data?

This is a great opportunity to seek clarification, develop new procedures, or possibly explore automations. For example, Aydan found a gap in capturing ongoing activity with clients. Firm leadership clarified the expectation that all major communications and interactions with clients were to be captured in the CRM system. And they took the time to define "major" as anything that would impact the business, giving applicable examples such as: learning a client received funding approval for a future project, a change in the client's business structure or leadership, personal information that everyone should know to better enhance the relationship with that individual (e.g., they like to hunt, dislike golf, have two young children and one in college, etc.). It is important to clarify these things because one person's definition of "major" might vary from that of someone else, which is how vital pieces of information slip through the cracks.

Data is an asset that needs to be protected, just like a business's finances. Every business has procedures in place regarding how employees handle money, whether it is a project manager creating a change order, an accountant issuing an invoice, or an estimator creating a bid. Unfortunately, not every firm takes its data management as seriously as it should.

When data is missed, lost, or goes uncaptured, the firm suffers. Referring back to the D&B survey shared in the previous chapter, one in five businesses lose revenue and clients due to incomplete data.[19] Do not be that firm!

REVIEW AND IMPROVE

After the process is mapped and the gaps are identified, it is good to pull others in to review the mapping so any silos can be addressed and any conflicting information resolved. Once the process map is complete, the improvements and changes can begin. Look for areas to remove double-data entry, reduce barriers of entry or bottlenecks, and utilize automations or workflow notifications.

These steps to map, identify, review, and improve can be done to document all your internal processes, from tracking a project from lead to completion and closeout, or tracking HR personnel functions from hiring through to the exit interview. Have you taken the time to document your project closeout process so every department, from accounting to marketing to operations, is on the same page?

Has marketing documented their content management process? Mapping content development from creation, editing, approval, and usage, outlining all the platforms and mediums being utilized. To fully maximize a piece of content, it should be used in a variety of ways, from articles in publications to social media posts, award submittals, and blog posts. Taking the time to document your firm's content management process ensures that your firm is maximizing the ROI on the time your staff invests in creating the material.

The list of internal processes to document is endless. These are just a few examples to get the ideas flowing. Head over to our website www.CRMorDie.com to download a mapping exercise to help you through this five-step process.

DO NOT SET IT AND FORGET IT

Process mapping requires monitoring and continual effort. It is an ongoing project, not a one-time project you complete, set aside, and never return to again. Your processes need to be maintained, reevaluated, tweaked, honed, and improved. Schedule time to do this on a regular basis and build in accountability to ensure that it happens. This is the only way to protect your valuable business assets.

Flip the Perspective

We have talked at great length about documenting internal processes. Now, let us flip things a little and look at the business from the perspective of your clients. Take a few minutes to jot down the journey your clients go through — from the time they first learn about your firm to the time they complete a project with your team.

Here are a few things to think to document your CX journey:

- **Prospect Stage.** How do your clients discover your company? Is it through referrals, Google searches of "best [architect, engineer, or contractor] in [your area or specific market]"? Or do they hear you present at organization events they attend?

- **Engagement Stage.** Once they encounter your firm, how do they engage with you? Through your website, social media, or publications? What is their impression of you; are you a thought leader and source of education or an industry leader with a wealth of experience? If they are just observing the business from a distance, are you aware of them?

- **Preparatory Stage.** Who makes contact first? Do you sit and wait, or do you have a proactive approach? Do you know who visits your website, and do you reach out? Do they have to complete a form to express interest?
- **Introductory Stage.** Once that first point of contact has been made, where is that captured? What message do they receive? How often do they hear from you after initial contact?
- **Proactive Stage.** When they have a potential project, do they have to contact you, or are you ahead of the game and reach out to them knowing they have a project you are best suited to assist with and have already positioned yourself as the obvious selection?
- **Project Kickoff.** Once you have won the project, what is the first thing they hear from you? Once the client awards your firm the project, hopefully the first thing they hear from you is not an invoice asking for their money. How is the handoff handled between BD and the operations team, is it a smooth transition from the client's point of view?
- **Project Duration.** Are client surveys conducted at certain milestones of the project to seek their perspective of how the project is going?
- **Project Closeout.** When the project wraps up, is there any closeout with the client or a gift that is given, or is it just a final invoice?
- **Continue The Relationship.** What is the communication cadence after the project is complete? Hopefully they hear from you regularly, so you are at the top of their mind when the next project comes around.

These are just some of the questions to ask as you create your CX mapping. The list could be expanded and made specific to your firm. Bring in other departments to broaden the viewpoint and get a full picture of what your clients experience when interacting with your firm.

Our CX Mapping Process

At CKearney Consulting, we deeply value our clients, strive to provide quality services, and prioritize our clients' experience. Accomplishing this can be challenging, especially given that our entire team works remotely, is spread throughout many geographic locations, and relies completely on virtual communication.

To prioritize our clients' experience, we dedicated one of our quarterly meetings to a half-a-day CX mapping exercise. We first created a rough, high-level outline, walking through the journey our clients take when engaging with our business.

Once it was sketched on the flip chart, we needed clarity on how we managed the process and flow as a team, so we dug into the terminology to get on the same page, clarifying the differences between a potential client, prospect, and lead. Everyone voiced the parts of the process they were responsible for, leaving gaps in parts of the process that needed to be claimed. We discussed how we keep track of the data at each step of the process, identifying what pieces of information are gathered, as well as when and where we intended that data to be stored. We also went a step further and outlined how that data would be used, measured, and reported.

Figure 5 shows the professionally illustrated version of our final CX mapping. Visit www.CRMorDie.com for a digital copy. This is the public version, however, there is an internal version with bulleted lists outlining each step of our CX process. It includes clear definitions of terminology to ensure that we are all on the same page and using consistent verbiage. Responsibilities and expectations are set for each step, clarifying the data that needs to be gathered, when it should be collected, where it needs to be entered, and by whom. We documented how the data would be used, allowing us to see how that small piece of information fits into the bigger picture.

Figure 5. CKearney Consulting's CX mapping

We track our CX process in our CRM system, of course! We keep a record of our opportunities, events, contacts, leads, interactions — everything pertaining to our CX process. Our CX informs our business strategy, so we are careful to keep records of as much as we can.

Get Everyone Involved

It is important for everyone to be a part of getting specific and mapping every piece of the process. It is a visual reminder of how crucial every single person's role is in the firm's CX journey.

Sometimes behind-the-scenes team members or those that are not client-facing question the importance of their work. Including the entire team in the mapping exercise and inviting them to take part in visualizing the process encourages them to see how each person contributes in meaningful ways, even if they are not directly interacting with clients. As the firm's leader, it is your job to make certain that each employee plays a role in the success of your clients' experience and the quality service you can provide.

Nailing down the specifics of your internal processes is necessary for success. However, do not forget to think externally. It is important to think about your clients' experience. Mapping the process that they go through when engaging with your firm can be eye-opening. Look at your accounting process from their perspective during the kickoff or closeout process. Taking the time to consider how your clients feel about the interactions they have with your firm fosters a trusted partnership.

Process Mapping Is the First Step

Documenting internal and external processes within the business is the first step in preparing for an integrated CRM solution. Human nature is to jump straight to the fix, to buy a CRM tool to solve your problems. We beg you to resist that temptation and instead focus on your process, preparation, and evaluation before the selection for a tool begins.

CHAPTER 4 KEY SELF-ASSESSMENT

- Do you have a process map documenting your CRM process?

- How do you focus your efforts, 90% on planning and 10% on the results?

- Do you document all your processes using this process: map, identify, review, improve, and monitor?

- Have you flipped the perspective and mapped the journey your clients go through while working with your firm, documenting your client experience (CX) process?

- Have you visited our website www.CRMorDie.com to access the additional resources?

5

Preparation Is Key

"Preparation is the key to success."
**— Alexander Graham Bell,
Inventor & Scientist**

CHAPTER 5 KEY TAKEAWAYS

1. Focus on your firm's internal processes for managing the client lifecycle from opportunity to project, documenting what happens each step of the way.
2. Have a change management strategy in place prior to selecting and implementing your integrated CRM solution. If you already have a tool in place, use change management strategies to increase user adoption.
3. Make sure you and your team are clear on the *why*. Why is your firm implementing this change *now*, and how will it help the business?
4. Get your data in order and prepped prior to starting the implementation of the CRM solution. If you have already implemented a solution, take time to review your data and the processes surrounding it.
5. Review your actions and those of your fellow leaders to ensure that you are supporting the effective use of your CRM solution and not being a barrier.

Case Study: Focus Internally First

Greg was Director of Marketing at Safron Architects, and Diann was Business Development Manager. For several years, they discussed the possibility of getting a CRM system and finally convinced senior management of the benefits, getting the budget approved to make the purchase the following year. They were elated to receive approval, but they had a problem; they were unsure what to do next.

When professionals like Greg and Diann know they need a CRM system, they often begin with software selection and turn to the internet to search for "the best CRM for AEC firms" or something similar. They look at the features offered by each of the top products and then try to figure out which one will meet their needs, or they quickly jump into a solution that an employee has used at a previous firm. Although these approaches are common, they are not the most effective long-term.

The first thing to do when preparing to buy an integrated CRM solution is to take the time to look internally at your firm and your processes. Remember, we use the term "integrated CRM solution" because we feel the best way to manage your client relationship is using a firm-wide system that is integrated into the flow of data to capture company, contact, pursuit, and project information. This integrated CRM solution should support managing client relationships, internal processes, and asset management.

System Integrations and Connections

Integrations with other programs and platforms are countless these days, as connections can be made using structured query language (SQL), plugins, application programming interfaces (APIs), data warehouses, and several other options. System integrations can assist with data flow, pulling information into the CRM solution or pushing out of the CRM platform and into other systems.

Some of the CRM solutions include a few selective integrations while charging an additional fee for other connections. Some integrations can be built into the product and activated easily, while others require advanced technical skills to configure or separate third-party products with added cost associated. Before you can know what system integrations you need, you must first be aware of how information flows through your business so you can find the best CRM solution that aligns with your organization.

Document How Data Flows Through Your Business

Understanding the lifecycle of a project is a good place to start. Documenting how data flows from a project lead to an opportunity or pursuit, and finally, to a secured project win, is important. It is vital to identify how each department tracks and manages data, as well as its impact on your clients and projects. Another important factor to consider is if there are any internal silos that exist within your business. You might be thinking, *Silos? No silos exist here!* After working on hundreds of implementations, we can tell you most firms have silos, and most remain unidentified until a firm begins prepping for a CRM system.

For example, if your marketers typically need to go to accounting to get final project and change order costs to include in RFP responses, you have a cost-data silo that is creating a barrier for marketing, causing inefficiencies. Sometimes, accounting can be protective of the information they give out and will delay giving this time-critical data, which could impact the marketing team's ability to respond accurately to a deadline, putting a pursuit win at risk. These kinds of silos or barriers need to be discovered early, addressed immediately, and resolved quickly.

Even if you have had your integrated CRM solution for years, we encourage you to document the flow of data through your business. Review your process mapping for potential silos and barriers, as they can persist well after your CRM has been implemented. Once they have been identified, remember to address them, and resolve them swiftly so your inefficiencies can be reduced.

Business Organization and Categorization

Another example of the business knowledge and understanding required to successfully select the right CRM solution for your firm is categorization and firm organization. Focusing internally first allows your team to be on the same page as to how your firm categorizes its work and its business prior to selecting a CRM system. How your business functions and how you want your data reported can determine which platform is best for your firm.

A good way to think about this is to ask yourself how you want to be able to "slice and dice" your data. Do you have territories, service lines, or divisions you want to see your pursuit data grouped by? Do you have vertical markets and want to know the firm's project history in those markets? Are you in more than one market? If so, can a pursuit or a project fall into more than one market or category? If it can, how are the fees or costs divided and reported? If the business has multiple locations, how do you determine which office chases a particular project?

One of our clients had a horrible situation happen prior to implementing a CRM system. Two offices both went after the same project and submitted competing proposals to a repeat client. To add insult to injury, they each offered different pricing — yikes! Not only did the CEO receive a call from the client to inform him of the two proposals, but the long-standing client also asked if they should pick the lower offer amongst themselves. As you can imagine, neither bid won, and the CEO never could shake the embarrassment of having two offices submit competing bids for the same project.

Several post-proposal conversations occurred to determine how to ensure such a catastrophic mistake never happen again. It was concluded that an integrated CRM solution would be purchased to provide transparent and consistent communication across all offices, allowing visibility into the opportunities that each was pursuing.

> *According to the SMPS Marketing 2022 report,*
> *the number one barrier to effectively using CRM was*
> *principals, seller-doers, and leaders not entering data.*[20]

Change Management Approach

Another important factor to consider when preparing to implement a CRM platform is if your firm has a change management framework in place. We know change management is a popular topic, and you have likely heard of the ADKAR, McKinsey, and Lewin models. One of our favorite models is Kotter's 8-Step Process for Change Management.[21]

In regard to using Kotter's 8-Step Process in conjunction with implementing an integrated CRM solution, here is an example of what that might look like:

- **Step 1: Create a Sense of Urgency.** Having the budget for a CRM does not necessarily make it an urgent initiative for the rest of your organization. However, in the previous example of a firm that submitted two proposals to the same client, this can create a sense of urgency to make sure such a problem does not happen again. We encourage you to lean into painful situations to capitalize on the internal sense of urgency they can create.
- **Step 2: Form the Right Team or Guiding Coalition.** Leadership involvement is key with implementing a new CRM as well as having key staff from marketing, BD, and IT. If your firm is integrating the accounting software with the CRM system, it helps to have a member from the accounting staff on the guiding coalition as well. The key to forming the right team is diversity across departments, tenure, and rank or position in the company.

- **Step 3: Form a Strategic Vision.** Make sure your team is clear on how implementing the CRM solution will change current and past processes, outlining what procedures will look like going forward and how these changes will make working together easier. To be most effective, the strategic vision and message must be unified and communicated clearly to all employees.

- **Step 4: Enlist a Volunteer Army.** Cultural change cannot happen with just the guiding coalition — more support is required. It is important to communicate the reason behind the CRM implementation, stress why the change is necessary right now, and invite others to join rather than mandate participation. Find ways to solicit support and sell the *why* for the change.

- **Step 5: Enable Action by Removing Barriers.** Sometimes, when rolling out a change, the biggest obstacle can be found between the ears of some of your colleagues. Quickly discover what limiting beliefs, fears, or anxieties might be standing in the way of adoption. It is important that everyone feel safe to voice their concerns so the guiding coalition can change the messaging and the way the vision is being communicated to help align your employees with the firm's needs. Another barrier can be the internal department silos that we addressed earlier. Whatever the barrier may be, addressing how it could block the overall success of the CRM implementation is critical.

- **Step 6: Generate Short-Term Wins.** When your firm begins to implement a CRM, setting key metrics for success along the way is helpful for the entire organization to see and be inspired by the progress being made. Short-term wins can be implementation milestones, adoption-focused, or accomplishment-driven. For example, wins during implementation could occur when configuration is complete, when data is migrated, or when training is completed. Adoption wins might be when a certain number of records are created in a specific time frame, or a set number of records are modified. Utilization wins could be when a pre-determined hit rate is reached or a contact to opportunity conversion rate is achieved. These short-term wins do not have to be complex; but they should be measurable to highlight that change is happening.

- **Step 7: Sustain Acceleration.** It is easy to let your foot off the gas when you start seeing those short-term wins, but that is absolutely the opposite of what you should do. The key is to continue to push forward, building and sustaining momentum. Consistently communicate the importance of the integrated CRM solution to meeting the firm's overall business objectives and strategic plan. A great way to make sure the CRM initiative continues to stay top of mind is to make it part of the agenda for the company-wide or all-hands meetings. Frequently report progress to sustain acceleration.

- **Step 8: Institute Change.** You will know your efforts have paid off when the CRM system and the process for updating, modifying, and reporting data from the CRM is engrained in the firm and no one remembers how you functioned before it was implemented. At this point, your integrated CRM solution and processes have become part of your firm's culture, and the entire initiative can be considered a success.

Clear Commitment to the Why

In Kotter's 8-Step Process for Change Management, creating the sense of urgency and forming a strategic vision go hand in hand with the underlying *why* of making the change.

When implementing a CRM solution, it is critical that from the CEO down, the entire organization is clear on why it is vital to the overall success of the firm. If senior leadership does not have a strong commitment to the *why* and the guiding coalition is not clear on how to communicate the *why*, the implementation has a greater chance of failure.

Sell the Why

Although Steve Jobs' management style was challenging for most of his employees to tolerate (Walter Isaacson's book, *Jobs*, cites many examples), one thing that was unquestionable was his ability to crawl inside the minds of his consumers and arrive at a simple explanation of how his newest product was exactly what each of us craved. On October 23, 2001, when introducing the Apple iPod, he led with, "1,000 songs in your pocket." Many people may not have exactly understood how much capacity 5GB was, but they certainly understood how cool it would be to have 1,000 songs in their pocket.[22]

When you start to zero in on your *why* for making change happen, the need for absolute clarity and focus cannot be overlooked. For example, your reason for implementing a CRM solution should not be, "We need to optimize the productivity of our marketing and BD teams to ensure that they only pursue work we have a good chance of winning." Instead, a better *why* would be, "We will be more selective with the projects we chase so we can focus our efforts on those we are best suited to win." Even better, we could shorten our *why* to, "We will use our CRM to be more strategic and win more work."

Get Clear on Your Data

No matter where you are on your CRM journey, it is important to organize your data, decide on naming conventions, and determine data responsibilities. If you do not have a CRM system yet, do not wait to do these things. Begin gathering data and having the necessary discussions to prepare for future decisions. If you already have a system but do not have good data organization, documented naming conventions, or clear responsibilities, take the time to establish them now.

It is important to be clear on where your data lives and how you intend to use it, gather it, and report on it prior to beginning implementation. Once you select a CRM platform and kick things off with the vendor, the implementation clock starts ticking. You need to know what level of support, if any, is provided by the vendor and if there is an expiration date tied to the assistance. You do not want to use up valuable time doing internal things like preparing data or having internal discussions about process that could have been handled previously. Implementation should focus on configuring the software and tailoring the system to meet your specific needs so users can utilize it on the designated "go live" or launch date.

Typically, vendors allocate six months or less for implementation support, and you do not want to stall out, lose traction, or kill adoption if decisions are being rushed or forced. If you are uncertain how some functions or features will work within the CRM platform, it is better to start the internal conversations to iron out as much as you can prior to implementation.

For example, every CRM requires that contact information be imported into the system. Knowing where all the records are prior to implementation will save time. Regardless of the system you select, you can proactively gather everyone's contacts from Outlook, your marketing database if you send email campaigns, and your accounting system if contacts are captured there as well.

Combine all the contact data into a master spreadsheet to remove duplicates, review company names, and perform a quality assurance/quality control (QA/QC) check. The important part of preparation is knowing where all the data is located, whether it is in multiple places on the servers, living in different systems, trapped in Outlook, on individual employees' machines, isolated in documents, etc.

The Devil Is in the Details

QA/QC is critical for data integrity, it is vital to the success of your business data flow and the systems you are utilizing. The key for QA/

QC comes down to details. For example, it must be determined how things like naming conventions will be handled. If the CRM system connects to your financial system, it is important that the company names align.

If, for example, accounting enters the client as The ABC Company and the CRM system has it listed as ABC Company, that is not a match. Therefore, the systems will not connect correctly, and a duplicate entry will be created. Make sure all departments — accounting and marketing, in this case — are clear on names and unique IDs for data that will be shared between systems, as both impact adoption and reporting.

Another detail to consider with data imports is how it is populated or structured within your spreadsheets. For example, we have seen clients whose data includes a contact's first name, last name, title, email address, and phone number all in the same cell. This format will not work for the QA/QC process and will not be compatible with any system import process. The data must be parsed out into separate cells.

Progress, Not Perfection

A word of caution on cleaning data: It is **never** going to be perfect!

When your team starts cleaning data in preparation for implementing your integrated CRM solution, it is critical that perfectionism does not stand in the way of progress. These examples are just a few of the kinds of data tweaks that can be made prior to beginning a CRM implementation. Tackling them ahead of time can help you during the implementation process and assist in a smooth implementation, especially during data migration. That said, the tweaks you could make to your data are endless, so set a specific window of time for data collection, population, and QA/QC. Once the window of time has ended, move forward with the data as it is. Focus not on perfection but on progress!

Combining Disparate Data Sources

Prior to beginning a CRM implementation, a huge time saver — and duplication eliminator — is to combine multiple data sources into a single spreadsheet prior to import.

Clients often ask if they can do multiple imports instead of having to combine files into a master spreadsheet. Many CRM providers do not like this approach for two reasons: It is taxing on their resources, and it inadvertently creates duplicates. Although some CRMs have excellent duplicate checking tools, it is good practice to review the data prior to import and make sure that duplicates are not being added from the start.

Data Population Is About Quality, Not Quantity

Although it is great to have copious data, it is not necessary to bring all of it in when implementing a new CRM system. In fact, one of the quickest ways to turn your colleagues off to the idea of adopting a new platform is to bring in data that is out of date and no longer useful.

When it comes to bringing in contact data, focus on contacts your firm is actively working with, has worked with in the past five years, or is on your holiday mailing list. But when it comes to opportunity data, start with active pursuits, possibly the projects won or lost during that current year for hit rate purposes. If your integrated CRM solution has a project management component, we recommend bringing in project data starting with the last seven to ten years. You can always add more data, but you do not want to get hung up trying to collect everything and miss the opportunity to make the greatest initial impact with the amount of data that is going to be most used on a regular basis.

CHAPTER 5 KEY SELF-ASSESSMENT

- Have you focused the necessary attention on your firm's internal processes for managing the client life cycle (lead to opportunity to project), and what happens each step of the way?

- Do you have a change management strategy in place?

- Are you and your team clear on the *why*? Why is your firm implementing this change *now*, and how will it help your organization?

- Is your data in order and prepped prior to your CRM implementation or for future imports to an existing CRM system?

- Have you reviewed your actions and those of your fellow leaders to ensure that you are supporting the effective use of your CRM solution?

- Have you visited our website www.CRMorDie.com to access the additional resources?

6

Evaluate and Select

"Directions are instructions given to explain how.
Direction is a vision offered to explain why."

**— Simon Sinek,
Author & Speaker**

CHAPTER 6 KEY TAKEAWAYS

1. Know what you want, why you want it, and how you will get it.
2. Leadership buy-in is critical and must be in place for your CRM to be successful.
3. Take the time to answer our list of questions before looking for integrated CRM solutions.
4. Stay in control and drive the selection process, as opposed to being driven by the process.

If you read the table of contents and skipped right to this chapter searching for the secret answer to "the best CRM platform to purchase," please stop reading and go back to Chapters 4 and 5.

Still here? Then we assume you have done the work to understand your firm's infrastructure, data, and processes. You have made plans for change management, and you have identified the champions that will help make this a successful launch. If you have accomplished all of this, the next step is to fully explore why your firm needs an integrated CRM solution and why it needs one now. The answer will dictate what system is right for your business.

Why Do You Need It?

As you can imagine, the answer to *why* you need a CRM can vary. There are endless reasons that drive the need for a CRM system. Some companies are focused on eliminating Excel and centralizing their data. Others need a more robust pursuit management tool. And some simply want a way to manage their contacts like a glorified Rolodex. (The many benefits of a CRM platform are outlined in Chapter 3 for those who need help figuring out why their firm needs an integrated CRM solution.)

We consider an integrated CRM solution to be a system that captures company, contact, and pursuit data but also is an asset management tool. Most commercial tools stop tracking information at the point of sale, which works for B2C businesses. However, for most business-to-business (B2B) companies in the professional service industry, the point of sale is when the relationship with the client begins, not when it ends. We need a system to track project data from the rumor of its existence to its conception, throughout the project to its completion, and continues to track client relationship building activity until the firm wins work with that client again.

> *There is no right or wrong answer to why*
> *your firm needs a CRM,*
> *but you must know your firm's why in order to*
> *find the right integrated CRM solution.*

Why Do You Need It Now?

Along with knowing why your firm needs a CRM solution, do not forget to figure out why you need it *now*. Referring back to Chapter 5, you will remember that creating a sense of urgency was step one of Dr. Kotter's change management process for a reason. It is critical to have that driving force to push you through implementation and into a successful future.

If there is a deadline in play — the contract on the existing technology is expiring, someone with a great deal of company knowledge and history is retiring, or the price for the system you want to purchase is only available for a limited time — that deadline needs to be communicated to everyone involved.

There might not be a deadline, but rather, a negative situation that you are trying to mitigate or prevent from happening again, such as the example we gave earlier of the firm that submitted two different proposals to the same client from different offices with different fees. It does not have to be that drastic; it could be that leadership is tired of seeing incorrect information in proposals and wants all the information coming out of one centralized location. If the project square footage is incorrect in a submittal, you can change it once, and it changes all the resumes and project sheets, ensuring that it will never be wrong again (if you are using a CRM with a publisher feature).

Whatever the reason, everyone involved needs to clearly understand what is pushing the need for a CRM solution to the top of the priority list. It could simply be that right now is the right time. If that is the case, pick a realistic timeline and set milestones to act as deadlines.

We all know projects without due dates do not get done. Be sure to allow sufficient time, typically four to six weeks, for the evaluation and selection process.

Three Simple Questions

In November 2018, Former Georgia House Democratic Leader Stacey Abrams gave a TEDWomen talk sharing three questions to ask yourself about everything you do. We feel her three simple questions can help start the evaluation process.[23]

1. What do you want?
2. Why do you want it?
3. How do you get it?

The answer to the first question seems easy in this case: You want a CRM solution. However, the real question is, "What problems do you want the CRM system to solve?" Simple, but not easy. Getting to the root of that question takes hard work and requires reviewing internal processes, as we outlined in detail in Chapter 4.

Question two is a little easier. Figure out why you want those issues resolved now and why you feel an integrated CRM solution is the answer.

Stacey tells us the final question to ask is, "How do you get what you want?" For us, we need to answer, "How does the CRM solution successfully integrate into your firm?"

The details of "how" might not fall on you, the leader, but it is important that all the employees know that you support the effort to make this new system a success. The questions that do impact leadership include, "How do you plan to use the data coming out of the CRM? What analytics and metrics are you wanting to see? How do you want the data displayed on dashboards? Do you want things categorized by market, office, divisions, profit centers, etc.?" Figure out what you want, why you want it, and how you get it.

Leadership Buy-In Is Critical

Just in case you really *did* skip ahead and did not heed our advice to go back and read Chapters 4 and 5, we will say it again here: The success of the CRM solution depends in large part on you, the leader.

You and your fellow leaders must demonstrate your buy-in and show support for the CRM process, the system, and data management for it to be taken seriously, to gain traction, and ultimately, to be a success. The SMPS Marketing 2022 research found that a lack of upper management driving CRM was one of the primary reasons for CRM ineffectiveness.[24] The great news is, you have the power to make the CRM a success instead of a hindrance.

Case Study: The Power of Accountability

Your leadership sets the tone and expectations for others to follow. Just like Jessica (the CEO of Phillips Lindell Contractors) did in Chapter 1 when she firmly explained that the CRM system was the new source of truth. Everyone in BD, marketing, and estimating was responsible for entering and keeping all pursuit and project data current and accurate. She explained why she needed the information and how critical it was to the company that the bonding report stay up to date. Clearly knowing the *why* allows you to articulate it to the staff and ensure adoption.

Right Team, Right Questions

We have addressed the initial three questions, but there are countless others that need to be answered. Head over to our website www.CRMorDie.com to download the full list. We will address some important ones here, but note this list does not cover them all. The implementation team you form should be the ones to review and respond to the full list.

1. **Interface.** How will the end users interact with the CRM solution that is selected? Will most users be on the web interface? Will they be in Outlook, engaging with an integrated feature that connects to the CRM? How mobile-friendly does it need to be (Android versus iOS support)? You want a solution that will meet your users where they already work for the highest rate of user adoption. The goal is for the CRM to smoothly slide into their existing workflow.

2. **Features.** Are there any dealbreakers that the CRM must have, like dynamic dashboards or an out-of-the-box integration with your financial system, or the ability to export every field of data? Does it need to have a built-in survey, email campaign, event management tool, or existing connection to the industry-leading platforms that offer those services? Do you want the CRM to provide goal setting, forecasting, revenue and/or workload projection support?

3. **User Interface (UI).** How important is the user interface? How user-friendly and intuitive is it? How customizable does it need to be?

4. **Specialization.** Does the CRM solution need to perform any specialized functions, like exporting documents to a specific platform such as Adobe InDesign or Microsoft Word?

5. **Integrations.** Does the CRM need to integrate with any other systems, such as financial, ERP (enterprise resource planning), Outlook, Intranet, Power BI, Constant Contact, Procore, or a lead service source like IMS, etc.?

6. **Categorization.** Can the system reflect how your firm is structured (offices, divisions, service lines, etc.)?

7. **Fee Structure.** Will you pay for just the licenses, or is there a mandatory implementation cost? When new modules and features are released, will they be included in your fee, or is there an additional fee? Will you pay per user or enterprise with unlimited users? Are there any additional upfront costs, annual fees, or

hidden fees? Is there a storage size limitation? If so, and it is exceeded, is there an additional cost?

8. **Community.** Do they have established user groups? Is there a good base of happy customers that connect and share ideas with one another?

9. **Support.** How is customer support? Is there regular online training, and if so, is it included or extra? Are there regular user conferences?

10. **Automations.** Most systems should have workflow capabilities to create notifications, set actions, make calculations, etc., but how detailed or well developed are they, and how much control and customization do you need?

Head over to our website www.CRMorDie.com to download a complete list of interview questions.

Drive, Do Not Be Driven

You would not go to a car dealership without knowing first what you want, or at least having something in mind. Without a clear understanding of what you need, what you want, and why, you run the risk of being sold a fully loaded car with all the bells and whistles — the salesperson could talk you into every unnecessary accessory under the sun, right down to a steering wheel heater. Then you get home, only to remember you live in Texas and do not need a heated steering wheel!

The implementation team should take the time to answer the previously mentioned questions before searching for the best integrated CRM solution. This will put you in the driver's seat. Ultimately, you want to drive the evaluation and selection process, not be driven by the salespeople at SaaS companies.

When you are driving, you are in control, and you can demand certain things. One of the things you should insist on is a list of references. Ask to talk to long-term, successful customers who currently use the features that are most important to you. Also, if you are doing integrations with your CRM, you want to speak to those references that have completed the exact same integration that you are requesting.

We want to stress that you need to meet with long-term users because those are the people who will be brutally honest about the product. They will have strong insights and let you in on the good, the bad, and the ugly. It is a waste of time to talk to a brand-new user who is regurgitating the sales pitch you have already been given, or a user who is satisfied with a product feature you have no intention of using. If a sales rep is unable to provide at least two or three good references that meet your requirements, that should be a red flag that maybe it is not the right fit for your firm.

It is also important to seek experts outside of the software company. Whether that means meeting with a group of superusers and picking their brains, looking for feedback on websites like G2 (a peer-to-peer review site), searching the chat boards of industry organizations like SMPS (mysmps.org), or consulting specialty firms like CKearney Consulting, who have valuable insight and knowledge, any and all expert insight you can gain is priceless and worth the time to find. You want to proceed with the confidence that you have all the data possible for selecting the best integrated CRM solution to fit your firm's needs. The wrong decision can cost you hundreds of thousands of dollars!

Interview Internally

In addition to seeking external feedback, interview your internal staff to fully understand how they intend to use the software. Hear firsthand from the end users to learn the pain points they want to remove and the problems they hope to solve with the CRM solution.

We have provided a few interview questions, but we encourage you to download the comprehensive list from our website, www.CRMorDie.com. After reviewing the questions, take time to customize them to be the most relevant to your firm.

1. **Contacts.** How are you currently capturing client contact data? Outlook, mobile, business cards?
2. **Leads.** What systems/technologies are you using to track leads/opportunities/pursuits? Excel, Outlook notes, a mobile or custom app?
3. **Process.** What is your process for getting leads? Getting referrals from existing clients, attending industry events, conferences, or trade shows, or simply retaining existing clients?
4. **Intel.** Do you have a regular meeting to discuss leads/pursuits? If so, is it a company-wide meeting, or is it limited to your office, market, or profit center? What is covered in those meetings? Who is responsible for capturing the data discussed, and where is it being stored and updated?
5. **Priorities.** What do you think should be your top three priorities for an integrated CRM solution? What are your personal goals or wishes for the CRM system?
6. **Needs.** What specific features are you looking for in a CRM? What needs does it need to satisfy? Asset or task management, activity, or pursuit tracking?
7. **Challenges.** What do you foresee being the biggest challenge(s) for the CRM to be successful? What could cause the CRM to fail?
8. **Accountability.** Do you see one person being responsible for the upkeep of the CRM tool, or will it be a group effort from all users? If you see it falling on one person, who do you envision that to be? If you see it as the responsibility of every user, how should each user be held accountable?
9. **Expectations.** What does a successful CRM implementation and launch look like to you? What are your expectations for the timeline to implement the system? What milestone(s) must be met for you to feel that the system has been implemented?

10. **Training.** How often do you feel users need CRM training for the system to be successfully adopted and used? What kind of training is most helpful to you? Online live sessions with a trainer? Short pre-recorded videos? In-person sessions over lunch? Half-day in-person training, and/or a written manual that can be reviewed independently?

Build the Matrix

Once you have collected all the data, you will be armed with a list of needs for the firm and the end users, which translates into a list of requirements for the CRM solutions you evaluate.

Cull through all the information you have gathered to form a selection matrix with your non-negotiable items in the first column. Each potential solution you bring to the table will get its own column and receive a rating corresponding to each item on the list. We have included a sample selection matrix to use as a baseline example. Take this and customize it to meet your needs and aid in the process of determining the top two platforms that will best fit your firm.

Selection Criteria	Option 1	Option 2	Option 3
Industry Specific			
Contact Management			
Project Lifecycle Tracking			
Opportunity Management			
Revenue Forecasting			
Mobile Accessible			
Outlook Integration			

Figure 6. Sample selection matrix

Begin the Search

Armed with a clear *why* statement — and an understanding of what the firm and end users need and want out of an integrated CRM solution — you are ready to begin the search for possible software solutions.

We recommend using industry resources like the SMPS Marketing 2022 publication, which mentions a survey with 300-plus participants comprised of engineering, construction, architecture/engineering, architecture, and other industry firm types. They shared the top five CRM platform products utilized at the time of the survey. JBKnowledge is another creditable resource to review, especially their annual ConTech Report, which includes the top CRM software being used in the construction industry.[25]

Since technology changes on a regular basis, we decided not to include a list of CRM solutions here. However, we have provided one on our website, www.CRMorDie.com, that will be kept up to date. Head there now for the list of our current favorites. It is our hope that this will aid in your selection process.

Rate the Options

Following the steps we previously outlined, take your selection matrix and put each potential solution at the top of a column. We recommend you limit this to your top four options, as more than four can make the process redundant and overwhelming. Properly researching and preparing for CRM selection is an investment, and you do not want to spend time gathering all the necessary data to populate the matrix on more than four platforms.

Using software websites, salespeople, system users, industry message boards, and all the other resources we have previously mentioned, populate each column by rating each potential product on every line item on the list. Remember, the line items are your non-negotiable needs and wants.

This approach allows you to evenly compare the platform options while not getting distracted by shiny features that are not essential to the success of your CRM system.

We have included a populated sample selection matrix below. This is only an example. Please take the selection matrix and customize it to meet your firm's specific needs.

Selection Criteria	Option 1	Option 2	Option 3
Industry Specific	✓	✓	-
Contact Management	✓	✓	✓
Project Lifecycle Tracking	✓	-	✓
Opportunity Management	✓	✓	-
Revenue Forecasting	✓	-	✓
Mobile Accessible	-	✓	✓
Outlook Integration	✓	✓	-

Figure 7. Sample populated selection matrix

Demo Phase

Before requesting demonstrations from your top two or three product selections, we recommend taking time to create an RFP, even if you never issue it. The exercise will be insightful as you prepare the questions you want to ask each company, define the information you want to receive, and outline your prioritized needs and desired features.

When you ask for a product demo, make it clear what you are looking to achieve and what you want to see in action. If possible, see if you can find a current user who can provide the demo in addition to the product sales team.

The demonstration phase is the precious bargaining window. You will not have this much power again until it is time to renew the contract or the licenses. Demand that each vendor take the time to present you with examples of exactly how the CRM will work for *your* company and meet *your* needs. Do not accept generic demos.

Selection Time

Reviewing the complete selection matrix might clearly reveal a CRM solution that best fits the firm's needs. With a clear winner, selection is easy. However, if it is not clear-cut, it is best to narrow it down to the top two platforms and present those options to your firm's leadership, explaining the differences between the options.

When it comes to selection, remember your *why* statement and check back in with all the previous work that is being done to document the process, prepare, and evaluate the options. In the event of a tie, reread the benefits outlined in Chapter 3 to clarify the differences between systems and help make your decision easier.

Honor Your Effort

You have put in the hard work, and you are ready to reap the reward of making the right decision for your firm. Celebrate and honor all the planning, preparing, process mapping, investigating, evaluating, digging, and questioning that has brought you to this moment. We are confident that you are now armed with the proper information and insights to make this data-driven decision!

CHAPTER 6 KEY SELF-ASSESSMENT

- Do you know what you want, why you want it, and how you will get it?

- Are you actively showing your support for the CRM process and the integrated solution? Do your fellow firm leaders also demonstrate their buy-in?

- Have you downloaded the list of questions, answered them, and documented the results?

- If you are evaluating systems, have you created and populated your selection matrix? Are you in control and driving the selection process, as opposed to being driven by it?

- Have you visited our website www.CRMorDie.com to access the additional resources?

7

—————

Implement Your Vision

"Begin with the end in mind."

— Dr. Stephen R. Covey,
Educator & Author

CHAPTER 7 KEY TAKEAWAYS

1. Begin with the desired results in mind, work backward to identify what you want out of the integrated CRM solution first, and let that drive the implementation process.

2. Preparing for a CRM tool is just as important as implementing and utilizing the tool.

3. Clean your data and break down silos prior to implementation for a smooth experience.

4. Proper and consistent training is the key to successful user adoption.

5. Focus your implementation using a tiered approach, rolling out core elements and aspects first and focusing on additional features later.

Case Study: The Cost of Being Underprepared

In Chapter 5, we talked about Greg and his excitement to finally be able to roll out a CRM system. While with his previous employer, he worked with the marketing team to roll out an integrated CRM solution that would integrate with their financial system, and it was an absolute disaster. He was adamant things would go smoothly this time around.

The previous firm had allowed its IT director to handle most of the system setup and configuration with little involvement from the marketing or accounting teams. Greg understood why the IT director did not want to involve either team; they could not agree on anything and would slow implementation down. There was a long-standing rift between accounting and marketing, and it seemed like nothing could be done to get the teams to work together.

Accounting did not understand why marketing needed the information they were requesting, and marketing did not understand why accounting made it so difficult to get the cost information they needed for proposals. These disputes would typically escalate until they were brought to the president of the firm for resolution. When the accounting team was told to provide marketing with the needed information, the accounting team held a grudge.

As Greg thought about this experience at his previous firm, he could feel his anxiety rising. But then he remembered that things would be different this time. He and Diann did the hard work before selecting the integrated CRM solution: They prepared for the CRM by adopting a change management framework, planned a communication strategy, discussed where key information about the CRM implementation would be stored so all the users could find it, and formed the right selection and implementation team.

The CRM team they formed to help select and roll out the integrated solution included the president, the accounting manager, and the IT director, while Greg was the representative for marketing and Diann represented all those with business development responsibilities. This team documented the internal workings of their organization when it came to how leads, opportunities, and projects were managed. They also took the time to fully map out the new CRM process, including how data would flow through the lifecycle of each new contact, pursuit, and project.

Between project pursuits and proposals, Diann and Greg spent countless hours organizing and cleaning the marketing and business development data. They combined information from many different locations and carefully scrubbed it for duplicates. Working closely with accounting, they made sure the client data (company names, addresses, and IDs) and the project data (names and IDs) aligned with what was in the accounting system. After all the preparation was complete, they were confident they were ready to select the best integrated CRM solution and begin implementation.

Implementation Kickoff

Greg, Diann, and the other internal team members were excited about the implementation kickoff meeting. The session was led by Piper, the CRM solution's implementation specialist, and she was joined by Paul, the CRM solution's integrations specialist. Piper started the meeting by outlining the flow of events, then detailed the implementation timeline.

They were told the entire implementation would take approximately four to five months based on the scope of services and their firm's needs. Greg was confident the implementation could be completed closer to the four-month mark based on how much preparation they did prior to selecting a product and kicking off implementation. During the meeting, they also reviewed the contract and the deliverables, confirmed the number of licenses, and discussed the additional system integration they purchased.

Greg presented the spreadsheets he and Diann had spent months cleaning up and preparing. He also shared a few sample reports that they wanted to generate out of the CRM system instead of continuing to spend time manually generating them. Piper was extremely pleased that Greg was able to furnish these spreadsheets at the kickoff, commenting that it would make their implementation easier than most, since they were so well prepared.

One thing Greg was surprised to learn during this initial call was that the CRM provider's implementation services expired six months after the contract was signed. That was something the CRM team had not planned on. Greg was thankful he and Diann had spent so much time planning and preparing the data, because those tasks alone took almost three months. If they had waited until the implementation kickoff to review their data and devise a clear plan, they would have lost valuable time and implementation support from the CRM provider.

> *Begin with the desired results in mind, work backwards to identify what you want out of the integrated CRM solution, and let that drive the implementation process.*

Configuration

During the CRM selection process, Greg and the CRM team decided they wanted a solution that was not complicated and would allow the internal staff to do all the necessary updates and adjustments to the system themselves. They made this clear to Piper, the CRM implementation specialist, so she would train them accordingly. The team was pleased to see how easy it was to make changes to their account on their own.

Piper kicked off the configuration call, announcing, "Few firms show up for the kickoff meeting with such clean data and have such a clear idea of the reporting they want. I have to say, this part of the implementation is running smoothly because you are all starting with the end in mind. It is important for firms to think about how they want the data to come *out* of the system. It is great that you have already given this so much thought."

Early in the preparation process, Greg and Diann knew it would be important for senior leadership to see the opportunity pipeline presented according to office, market sector, and practice area. By working alongside accounting, they were able to align the data they wanted in the CRM system for forecasting and marketing with how accounting viewed their data.

During one of the configuration sessions, Greg asked about the ability to change some of the value lists as their firm changed and grew. Piper showed him where in the system the values could be changed to meet their needs. The firm was anticipating an opportunity to acquire one of its competitors and would need to make changes when that happened. It was still in the early stages, but during the planning process, they discussed the importance of a flexible CRM platform that could absorb the new firm's data as easily and seamlessly as possible.

Financial System Integration

After the initial system configuration was complete, it was time to begin mapping and setting up the integration between the financial system and the CRM.

During data preparation, Greg and Diann found discrepancies in the dollar fields for project records, as well as differences in final cost data across the marketing and accounting departments. They were able to raise these issues during their planning sessions, which resulted in productive discussions where the accounting department was able to explain to the marketing team which fields they used in the accounting system and why.

For a long time, Greg and Diann thought the accounting team was not populating key data points, when in fact, the information was just in a different module of the system. Having these discussions during the planning sessions made the team feel comfortable, and they were able to move forward as a united group. It was vital that the team be unified going into the mapping discussions with the CRM provider's integration team.

This phase of the implementation was led by Paul, the CRM solution's integrations specialist. At the conclusion of the first integration meeting, Paul shared some feedback with the Safron CRM team.

"Usually, when we have these mapping meetings, accounting is unsure why marketing needs certain information, and marketing becomes defensive," said Paul. "I typically spend most of the time working with people to find where data lives in the system so we can pull it over to the CRM. Then the process is usually delayed, as most of the fields that marketing wants to bring over are not consistently populated in the financial system. It is great that you guys have already had these conversations and know which fields of data you are looking to bring into the CRM system. Because of the work you have done ahead of time, this is going to make the rest of this process go much smoother and faster."

Paul wrapped up the meeting by explaining that he would complete the mapping documentation, outlining each field of data that will transfer from the accounting system to the integrated CRM solution, and then he would send it to the Safron team to review. That, he clarified, is the time to make changes and ask any clarifying questions. After the CRM team approved the mapping, Paul and his team would write the code for the queries to over the data from the accounting financial system into the CRM.

He outlined that the first run would populate the UAT (user acceptance testing) account instead of the live production account that users were already actively using to track their contact and pursuit information. The UAT refers to a copy of the live account that is used for testing and trying out changes before making them live for all users. The first migration would only bring over data from the five sample projects they had selected to test the integration and make sure data was populated where the team intended.

The final step required the CRM team members to log in to the UAT environment and validate the sample data, including reviewing the information to ensure that it was populated where it should be and that it worked in those fields. If something was missing or things needed to change, this was the time to make those requests. After the team approved the mapping, Paul and his time would do a full run to bring the complete project history over to the live production account.

The team appreciated Paul's thorough explanation and was excited to take on the next step in the process. A few days after their initial meeting, they received an email informing them that sample data was ready in the UAT environment. Greg and Diann were excited and jumped into the CRM system's testing account.

They were elated to see project data from the financial system neatly integrated into a centralized solution the entire company could access. Greg responded to Paul to confirm that the data migration was a success. He stated that they were satisfied with how the fields were populated in the CRM system and granted permission to make the integration "live." With this approval, Paul set the integration to run, transferring the firm's project history into the production site, the CRM account all the users regularly access.

This was a big win not only for Greg but the entire CRM team. It had taken months of hard work and a good deal of collaboration to get to this point, so they took time to celebrate. In honor of reaching this important milestone, the team headed out for an extended lunch together.

Initial Communications Campaign

While implementation, configuration, and integration were underway, Greg and Diann created an internal communications campaign. The first step informed the employees that an integrated CRM solution had been researched and selected, and implementation had started. This was accomplished with a company-wide email explaining why the firm needed a CRM system, why they needed one now, and how it would be utilized. For transparency, the email also included a timeline outlining the full implementation schedule.

The campaign outlined several future emails to share the CRM process to make it clear what role each department would play, creating clear expectations for how everyone would contribute. Training schedules were provided, along with a synopsis of what materials would be covered and who was expected to attend.

It was Diann's idea to take five-to-ten minutes at the weekly staff meeting to give CRM updates. She started with a ten-minute presentation on "What is a CRM and Why We Need One." Each week, Diann updated the entire firm on the progress of implementation. She also sent a follow-up email summarizing key aspects of the implementation and directing employees to a SharePoint site containing more information.

For the first weeks, Diann received "crickets" from the employees, and it seemed like people were not interested in the new CRM process or system. Until two proposals were submitted to the same client, that is! (This incident was discussed in greater detail in Chapter 5.) After that experience, engagement increased, and several employees started asking questions following Diann's CRM implementation update at the weekly meetings.

Her colleagues asked questions like, "How will the new CRM ensure that we do not duplicate efforts?" and, "Is the new CRM like big-brother management?" After some of these questions, it was extremely helpful to have the president jump in and reiterate the *why* for the change.

He explained, "We are doing this so we can be smarter with the best resources we have — that goes for each of you. Tracking our pursuits, associating personnel with those pursuits, and tracking what each of you is doing on them ensures that we do not duplicate internal effort and go after the same project. This process will also allow us to have a more accurate picture of our pursuit pipeline and help us plan ahead better.

"We do not want you to think of this as a 'big brother' approach. Instead, see this as a safeguard against miscommunication, a way for us to increase our efficiency and increase our data-driven decision-making, basing our decisions on facts instead of gut feelings. I believe this will allow us to handle the ebbs and flows of the market much better.

"Remember, the goal of having a well-defined CRM process and a properly populated CRM system is so we can turn the data from the CRM into knowledge and insights which we will convert to our competitive advantage. After all, information is power and currency. The businesses that understand that will thrive and not perish."

Training and Documentation

With data in the system, the team was now ready to start using it. That meant it was time to start training and rolling out the platform to employees.

The CRM team chose a train-the-trainer approach, which meant Piper, the CRM Implementation Specialist, trained Greg and Diann on how to use the system with the intention that they would then train the rest of the users. Greg was excited about this approach because it would give him and Diann a chance to play with the system prior to the entire firm rollout and the opportunity to document aspects of the software that were unique to their firm.

At Greg's previous firm, the CRM provider had conducted separate trainings for each user group: BD, marketing, and project managers. Although this seemed like a good idea at the time, the CRM provider was not well versed in the nuances of their business, so some key features and data capture requirements were left out. During this implementation, however, Greg decided to utilize a train-the-trainer approach, since he was familiar with the internal workings of the firm and could control how the training was delivered.

Diann took extensive notes during the training sessions with Piper and was able to use the SharePoint site she built to store all the training documentation she created. Piper was able to provide Diann with some great starting points for system documentation that could be modified to their system.

Here is the list of documents they created after the training:

- **Key Terms.** A document clarifying the definitions of terminology used in the CRM process and system.
- **Process Guide (Flow Chart).** A document visualizing and explaining how leads, opportunities, and projects are tracked and managed within the organization in conjunction with the CRM and financial system. This included a data flow chart showing how information moved through business operations, highlighting data collection points as well as notes documenting how the data would be used, tying it back to *why* it is needed. It also included the data policies and standards.
- **CRM User Guide.** A step-by-step guide showing how to create and modify each type of record in the system: company, contact, lead, opportunity, project, and personnel. Other items such as an activity log, a basic report, a dashboard, and a dashboard widget were included.
- **Integration(s) Guide.** A document illustrating how all system integrations work in conjunction with the CRM solution. For Safron, that included the connection from the accounting system to the CRM and the Outlook add-in, as well as the third-party integration pushing contact data to the email campaign tool.
- **Expectations and Responsibilities Matrix.** A chart documenting each team member's data role(s), tasks, and responsibilities regarding the CRM process and system. The expectations were included, stating how often users should be in the system and by what key performance indicators (KPIs) they would be measured.

Training and System Rollout

There are five best practices we recommend for CRM training sessions. If you follow these, you will set your firm up for success. These principles will lead to proper and consistent training, which is the key to successful user adoption.

1. Always start your training with your *why*!
2. Make training sessions role- and/or topic-specific.
3. Training should be frequent and consistent.
   Make it a cultural norm.
4. When possible, address multiple learning styles.
5. Keep it short and sweet.

In alignment with best practice number two, the CRM team decided to follow three role-based user training sessions: BD, marketing, and executives. First, each group was notified well in advance of the trainings, and all the resources Diann developed were emailed and included in the training calendar invites. Each user was asked to review the materials *prior* to the training sessions.

For the initial one-hour training session, Greg began with a recap of the *why* and made sure each team member was comfortable with the resources provided prior to training. He confirmed that each user had access to the system and knew where all the supporting resources were located.

During training, Greg focused on the key modules important to the specific user group being trained. He made sure to address multiple learning styles by first doing a demonstration and providing a printed manual. He then had the users get into their own accounts and navigate the system to help those who learned best by doing it themselves. He made sure to leave enough time for questions and ended every training with homework assignments. Users had one week following training to enter their data in the system and needed to inform Greg once it was complete.

The BD users had to review the contacts in Outlook to those in the CRM system. They had to create and enter any missing contacts into the system. They were also responsible for reviewing the pursuits in the account and entering any new or missing opportunities. Marketing reviewed the project data, entered any missing information, and corrected any errors. They also uploaded the final proposals to the opportunity records for all the pursuits the firm won that year. The executives had to review and provide feedback on the dashboards and reports the CRM team had created.

To encourage users, they were rewarded with an Amazon gift card after they completed their homework. Since the employees were not expecting this, it helped keep things positive. Plus, it created a little buzz within the organization.

The second round of training combined the BD and marketing users, as Greg touched on reporting and dashboards. This was already covered in the first session for the executive users, so they were not included in this round of training. For homework, users were required to create their own report and dashboard. There was a higher completion rate and faster turnaround for homework assignments after the second session, likely due to the surprise gift card when homework was completed. For this round, users who successfully completed the exercise on time were rewarded with a second Amazon gift card, much to their delight.

With the initial training sessions complete, Greg changed the cadence to a biweekly lunch-and-learn held every other Thursday. He understood that training should be frequent and consistent. He worked to make it a cultural norm. Users from all groups attended together and had the opportunity to ask general questions that came up as they were using the system. Greg would answer the questions during lunch training, do a live demonstration of anything new in the system or show anything that needed clarification. He would also review the Expectations and Responsibilities Matrix.

Following the sessions, he would incorporate the notes into the related documentation on Diann's SharePoint site. Greg emailed a recap to attendees and referred them back to SharePoint so everyone was continually directed to a resource that could support them as they increased their knowledge in the platform.

After two months of lunch-and-learns, attendance started to wane, so Greg decided it would be best to move to a once-a-month schedule and change it to a short and sweet 30 minutes. When Greg made this change, he also changed the format. During the monthly sessions, Greg started off with a quick refresh on key areas of the system and provided an overview of new features that were released since the last get-together. He then turned the rest of the session over to another user.

Users took turns presenting their favorite features to the group, sharing how they used it, what they got out of it, and how it had helped them. They would answer any questions and conclude by picking another user to present the following month. A pattern quickly emerged that the person absent got picked as the next presenter — this really helped attendance and, naturally, kept users incentivized to attend.

A Word of Caution Regarding Implementation

During his first CRM implementation with his previous employer, Greg learned the importance of prioritizing features in order of importance.

Implementing all features and modules at once proved to be too much for users to absorb. Most CRM solutions have a long list of features, modules, and additional integrations that make sense to implement in the long run but not during the initial implementation. Trying to bite off more of a new system than you can chew can doom the adoption before it starts.

With the second implementation experience, Greg wanted to achieve a higher rate of CRM adoption. To accomplish this, he followed a change management framework (similar to Kotter's 8-Step Process mentioned in Chapter 5) and focused on rolling out the most critical features first, letting less important aspects be introduced at a later time.

It is important to structure your implementation so that you achieve short-term wins early and often. If you couple that with celebrating the milestones the CRM team achieves, you can guarantee the rollout of your CRM system will be a huge success.

CHAPTER 7 KEY SELF-ASSESSMENT

- Have you spent adequate time deciding what your desired results are so your team can work backward to identify what you want out of the integrated CRM solution?

- Have you allocated the necessary resources to properly manage your client relationships, your CRM, and your data management processes?

- Does someone in the firm regularly clean your data and review it for silos that might be negatively affecting the business?

- Do your users receive proper and consistent training on the integrated CRM solution, covering the core elements, the new features, and how to best utilize the system for your firm?

- If you are planning a CRM solution implementation — or are in the process of implementing one — have you set realistic expectations using a tiered approach, or have you tried to execute too much too fast?

- Have you visited our website www.CRMorDie.com to access the additional resources?

8

Execute Your Vision

"Every action you take is a vote for the type of person you wish to become. No single instance will transform your beliefs, but as the votes build up, so does the evidence of your new identity."

**— James Clear,
Author of Atomic Habits**

CHAPTER 8 KEY TAKEAWAYS

1. An integrated CRM solution is a tool to help humans, not replace them. Client relationship management is about process and people; it is not about a piece of technology.
2. Everyone in your firm must understand the story that data is telling, especially the business leaders.
3. Team members need to be empowered to use data.
4. It is vital that you and your fellow leaders hold your staff accountable, using data positively and not punitively.
5. Utilizing a centralized database will save the company money and increase business efficiencies.
6. Celebrate adoption and utilization successes for each accomplishment, milestone, and step along your CRM journey.

In Chapter 3, Patrick successfully convinced Brendan, President of Brueggemann Civil Engineering, of the benefits of using an integrated CRM solution. As the VP of Operations, Patrick knows that the adoption of anything new starts at the top, making leadership buy-in critical. For this reason, he was strategic with his first company-wide email about the new CRM process and system. In the email he:

- Explained the benefits and encouraged participation in the CRM system.
- Set expectations and responsibilities, including holding team members accountable to their KPIs.
- Described how this will empower doers to become doer-sellers.
- Expressed that the CRM tool will provide everyone access to centralized and transparent data.

In this chapter, we will walk through how Patrick and his team tackled each of these objectives to accomplish the successful adoption of a new CRM process and system.

Case Study: Use the System to Drive Adoption

Patrick closed the door to the conference room and announced it was time to begin the weekly BD and marketing meeting. Everyone took their seats and began looking at the projection screen, which showed Patrick's CRM account. Once everyone set their attention on the list of opportunities displayed, Patrick reminded the group, "We are only discussing pursuits that have been entered in the CRM."

With that statement, Patrick heard Zack flip open his laptop and begin typing. There were a few chuckles as team members could see Zach trying to quickly add opportunities to the system. Patrick smiled and thought to himself, *Well, at least he is getting the information into the system.*

Patrick glanced back at the screen and was pleased to see all the pursuits entered. He recalled previous meetings in which everyone had come with printouts of their individual Excel document with only their opportunities. As a result, people would zone out when fellow team members talked about opportunities not related to their own department or projects.

Now, with everyone's opportunities entered in the CRM system, there was a greater sense of transparency and shared commitment. Patrick sorted pursuits by dollar value, beginning the weekly discussions with the largest opportunities, which gave everyone a competitive spirit since they wanted their opportunities to be discussed first. It also held everyone accountable for entering a dollar amount on the pursuits. Otherwise, their opportunities would immediately fall to the bottom and be ignored.

To capitalize further on the competitive nature of his team, Patrick increased the CRM budget to accommodate rewards for employees who adopted the platform. Marketing launched competitions for "Most Contacts Entered" and "Most Opportunities Updated" and rewarded the winner(s) with a gift card or lunch. During the weekly BD and marketing meetings, Patrick was delighted to see the new and updated opportunity data and felt that the adoption strategy and incentives were working well.

Patrick was midway through the list of opportunities when he noticed that many of the proposal due dates fell around the same time: roughly 45 to 60 days out. Having that many deadlines at once impacts the marketing team's capacity. Patrick had been debating whether the firm needed to hire an additional marketing coordinator, but this insight made it clear that it needed to happen — and soon.

After the meeting, Patrick asked Erin, the marketing manager, to stay behind and discuss the forecasted workload. Erin immediately smiled and said, "I am happy you want to discuss the proposal load because it looks like we will be over capacity in a month and a half. We have numerous deadlines the week of August 15."

She went on to say, "The marketing team is glad to have these opportunities, and we especially enjoy how easy they are to organize and track within the new CRM tool, but we need to discuss an increase in staffing or a reduction in the number of proposals we are pursuing. I have always wanted a way to quantify and show how busy the marketing department is, and now everyone can see it so clearly!"

Erin was an early adopter of the CRM and was involved with many aspects of the implementation. She led the internal email campaign that generated buzz about the CRM, created a SharePoint site to house key documentation, and facilitated the data entry and cleanup of the project data. After the CRM was fully implemented, Erin continued to send weekly emails to all users with tips on how to use and maximize key features of the platform.

Although CRM adoption can be a challenge, the impactful insights gained by successfully utilizing a CRM platform far outweigh the work it requires. As shown in the previous example, even late-adopters like Zach see the value of an integrated CRM solution when change is supported from the top down, adoption is incentivized, and all employees are held accountable for embracing the changes. It is also beneficial to highlight the successes of early adopters like Erin and encourage your CRM champions to share the benefits of the platform with those who are hesitant.

Accountable to Key Performance Indicators (KPIs)

After seven months of using the CRM, the team at Brueggemann Civil Engineering gained familiarity and comfort with the system. More importantly, Patrick saw a shift in mindset as the team began trusting the data in the system. He and the senior managers began preparing for review season, which they knew struck fear in most of the employees at the firm. Patrick, on the other hand, was excited about this year's review process because they could rely on the data from the CRM system to create realistic and achievable goals for the team.

Patrick decided to conduct the first review with Zach. He knew Zach was initially hesitant about using the CRM data to create his KPIs. Despite the pushback, Patrick knew the CRM provided real data they could use as the basis for goal setting instead of relying on personal feelings about what an employee wanted, hoped, or intended to accomplish the following year.

Zach stood outside Patrick's office in nervous anticipation of his annual review. He took one last deep breath and knocked on Patrick's door.

Patrick looked up from his computer. "Hi, Zach. Please have a seat, and we can talk about all of the good things that have happened this year." Zach relaxed at this greeting, and they began to review his performance.

"Zach," Patrick began, "I know we have implemented some changes lately, especially with the rollout of the new CRM process and system. I want to thank you for making an effort to use the system. We have data now that can help us review the work you have completed this year with your team and gives us the transparency to see what you all have in your pipeline. This is exciting and shouldn't be feared."

Zach replied, "I have to admit, I was initially hesitant to embrace the system. However, I'm glad I did because once I looked at the data, I was genuinely shocked at the insights I gained! Honestly, that's why I'm nervous about this review. The data doesn't look so good.

"When my team started looking at the clients we were working with, the work they have coming up, and how profitable our past jobs with them have been, I was really surprised. In fact, I was angry for a little while. My team was working so hard, but it was clear after looking at how much we were making and what we forecasted that we were spinning our wheels and not getting anywhere."

Patrick was taken aback. This was a different side of Zach than he had seen previously. "I know it is hard to look at your clients and your projects this way," he said, "but in the long run, I think it is going to help you and your team grow your client base in a way that will be more profitable, and also less stressful."

Zach quickly jumped in. "I completely agree! I am looking forward to setting new goals for myself as well as for the team. We are ready to make some changes. For a while, I have been focusing primarily on retail. I thought if we served the client well, they would take care of us, but I was wrong. We gave several clients extra hours, and they still turned around and bid out most of the work. It has been so frustrating. Seeing the amount of work we have been doing compared to our actual profits started to really get to me.

"I want to make some changes this year and focus more on the healthcare and higher education markets. Several of my direct reports have some good relationships that we have not taken advantage of, and I would like to shift our attention to those going forward. I also want to make sure that I am tracking our progress on a more consistent basis. I want the team to see how well we are doing. During one of our training sessions, Erin showed us how to customize our dashboards in the CRM. I think this could be an effective tool to make sure the team can see where we are as we strive toward new goals. Can you help me create a better dashboard to track our new goals for next year?"

The review took a pause, and Zach logged in to the account to show Patrick the widgets currently on his dashboard. With a little discussion, the two came up with the dashboard in Figure 8, which helped support the data story Zach was telling.

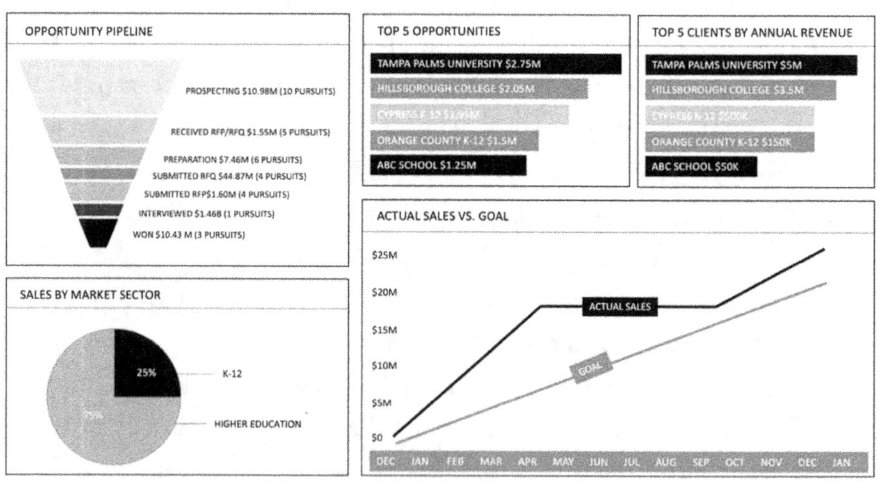

Figure 8. Sample dashboard

As you can see, when Zach looked at the company pipeline and sales by market sector, it was clear that retail was not strong. This insight required action, which Zach was proactively taking, and Patrick was elated.

Patrick and Zach spent the remainder of the review working together to create new goals for Zach and his team. Some of the metrics were vague, or even generalities, since Zach wanted to pursue two new markets they had not worked in previously. They decided to be conservative in their estimates for work that would be earned in the next year. One thing was clear, though. Both Patrick and Zach left the review feeling better about the direction of the department than either had anticipated.

Understanding Dashboard Widgets

As your team starts to dive into your CRM dashboards and widgets, you will realize that there is nuance to how you should approach this. Two people can look at the exact same graph or chart and come away with two different conclusions.

One person could look at the pipeline widget in the upper-left corner of Figure 8 and see the shape of the funnel and conclude that the company is in a great spot, assuming that the shape is dynamic and controlled by the dollar value of each stage.

Another person could look at the same pipeline widget and see that the shape is static and will remain a funnel regardless of the data. Upon further review, they could also notice that the height or thickness of each section is tied to quantity (number of pursuits in that specific stage) and not distributed by dollar volume.

Either way, someone needs to understand how much revenue it takes to keep the lights on, how much it takes to make a profit and work backward to determine — based on hit/win rates, interview rates, etc. — how much needs to be in the early pursuit stage so you can win enough work to keep the doors open and make a profit.

Similarly, every employee should understand the KPIs they are working toward and expected to meet. Each team member needs to be clear on their CRM and data responsibilities and know that they will be held accountable to meet them. Visit the www.CRMorDie.com website for a sample list of key performance indicators.

Empower The Doers to Become Doer-Sellers

When a firm uses a CRM to its full potential, everyone becomes part of the sales team. Patrick suspected this, but he saw it in action as he walked past the receptionist's desk and overheard a conversation between his receptionist, Richard, and one of their clients, Jared.

"Hey, Jared, it's great to see you. We have not seen you in months, but I hear the Pinnacle Park project is moving right along. I know Jacob's team is proud of the progress it is making."

As Patrick peeked around the corner, he saw Jared smiling as he said, "You're absolutely right, it's coming along really well. Actually, that's why I am here. There are a few more details we need to wrap up on the next phase, but we are close."

Richard continued, "That is great to hear. I also wanted to let you know I heard about your son's recent illness, and I am happy to hear that he is doing better."

Jared's face displayed a little surprise, followed by appreciation for the comment and the concern. "Wow, that is very kind of you. Thank you. He is doing much better. It has been a rough couple of weeks, but I appreciate your support."

Richard and Jared's exchange demonstrated a key principle: Business developers can no longer be the sole relationship managers. If they are, the organization loses vital connections when BD team members leave the firm. Plus, this interaction proves that clients feel more valued when more than just the BD or sales team knows them.

Business developers can no longer be seen as the sole relationship managers. Everyone in the business must see themselves as relationship builders.

When Jared visited the office and Richard was able to access the CRM platform to identify Jared's project, the status, and key information about the firm's relationship with Jared, it allowed Richard to build rapport. Richard had seen a note entered two weeks previously, indicating the project had incurred a one-week delay while Jared traveled back and forth to the hospital to visit his son. The project manager, Jacob, also updated the record to reflect when Jared's son recovered.

When everyone at your organization has access to client information, they can leverage this information to enhance relationships. Harnessing the power of what you know about your clients empowers your team to provide multiple touchpoints for each relationship.

Another way your team can stay in touch with your clients is through client interests. CRM platforms are great tools for storing contact preferences. For example, value lists that are configured by contact interests can be immensely helpful: Hunter, Golf Enthusiast, Clay Pigeon Tournament Lover, Bowling Fan, Avid Runner, and so on. Making changes like this to the out-of-the-box CRM platform can be a great way to help your team make lasting bonds with contacts. By connecting with clients on relevant interests, you solidify the relationship.

Harness the Power of Centralized Data

Jack, one of the Senior Project Managers at Brueggemann Civil Engineering, recently worked on several RFP responses with Erin. He noticed there had not been as many emails and phone calls requesting information as there had been on previous submittals. He was concerned that he had not heard from Erin as much as he normally did, so he decided to stop in and check on things.

Erin was working on binding a proposal when Jack walked up to talk with her. "Hi, Jack," she said. "I am just working on binding the RFP responses for Blanca Partners. Man, that was a tough one — 250 pages! I am glad to have this one finished. Can I help you with something?"

"Well," Jack said, "I actually wanted to talk to you about proposals. I was listed as Senior Project Manager for several of the pursuits we have in the pipeline, and you usually reach to me for information, but I haven't heard from you. I know I have been busy, but if you need my help, I will dedicate the time to get you any project information you need for the RFP response."

Erin smiled and said, "That is nice of you to ask. I will need you to review the drafts once they are ready. The reason I haven't reached out to you lately is because all the information I used to get from you is in the CRM system. I have a place to track it all now. All the information I need for our proposals is there, since it's integrated with our financial system and updated on a nightly basis. That means I have all the real-time data I need without having to make repeat requests to you or others."

Jack laughed. "Wow! You mean I am not going to have to mark up the same information over and over on proposal documents? Nice! I am so happy you have access to all that data now."

If your team completes proposal responses, this case study anecdote may resonate with you, as you have probably had to repeatedly update the same information. This kind of duplicate work is not only annoying and inefficient but is also costly. Combine the hourly rate for just a few of the project managers at your firm, and you can see how expensive it is to update information multiple times.

Once your firm fully commits to the new CRM process and shifts away from Excel spreadsheets driving everything to be entered into the centralized CRM database, the efficiency and cost savings are incredible.

Celebrate the Wins

Another way to ensure continued CRM adoption at your firm is to celebrate any and all wins.

No matter how big or small a win is, bring attention to it. There is science behind this thought process. It is neurological and should be something you do personally and professionally. Liz Guthridge shares some insight on this in a Forbes article titled *Recently Succeed At Something? Celebrating Is Good For Your Brain.*

> *As an example, say you hit a project milestone on time and on budget and note your accomplishment. You get a hit of dopamine, the "feel-good" chemical. Dopamine acts as a neurotransmitter, sending signals to other neurons that serve as a pleasurable reward. These neurons that fire together now start getting wired together in your brain.*
>
> *When you experience the dopamine reward, your brain pays attention to what you did to deserve your "feel-good" moment. That includes the brain calculating what's needed to repeat that action and move toward achieving your goals. The dopamine also plays a role in regulating your attention, learning, and movement.*
>
> *Recognize and embrace the science of celebration. Acknowledging and celebrating your accomplishments helps you and your brain make a strong connection between the achievement you're celebrating and the behaviors that got you there.*[26]

We know it is not always possible to stop and celebrate every win *every* time, but we should strive to make it a goal to do so 75% of the time, at least. For some inspiration, we will look at a couple of ways Patrick and his team celebrated to ensure their efforts continued to be successful.

- **Review Contacts Annually.** Historically, Erin hated the fall because it meant the conversations about holiday cards and holiday gifts for clients would start up. This year, however, was different. She had a process and a system that would make this a smooth and pleasant experience for everyone.

  In September, she created a thermometer graphic with the total number of contacts at the top with four section breaks marking each quarter's goals. She blew it up and mounted it on a board in the break room for everyone to visualize how the cleanup project was progressing. Patrick announced at the marketing and BD meeting that there would be a celebratory party (pizza, ice cream, a food truck, whatever they wanted) once they filled the thermometer and every contact was reviewed and up to date.

  Everyone was so excited about earning the celebration that they met their goal two weeks ahead of schedule, which made Erin very happy and reduced her typical holiday stress. The staff made comments about not wanting to wait another year to repeat the party, so they approached Patrick about doing something similar in March. He agreed, of course, since that meant contacts would be reviewed at least twice a year.

- **Share Success Stories.** The interaction between Richard, the receptionist, and Jared, the client, made such an impact on Patrick that he told the story at the staff meeting. He took five minutes to celebrate Richard's efforts to talk to Jared about his project and his son. He even gave Richard the mic to allow him to share how he had gotten all the valuable information from the CRM system, and Richard gave a shout-out to Jacob for adding the note in the system.

  After that meeting, Patrick heard a lot of comments thanking him for sharing the story and taking the time to celebrate the team members. Some said it was eye-opening to see the direct impact CRM can have on clients. This encouraged Patrick to continue to share success stories during staff meetings.

Change the Trajectory of Your Business

Engaging a team to use a CRM, holding team members accountable for using the platform, and continuing to drive everyone to the centralized data is a large undertaking.

Keep in mind that it can sometimes take up to 18 months for a process or software change to be fully adopted, so be patient during the process. To fully execute your vision, it is important to reiterate that a CRM is a tool to help humans, not replace them. It is job security, not job replacement.

A CRM empowers every employee to become a relationship builder. It allows for transparency in the business, and it gives marketers their job back so they can be strategic with their time instead of hunting and gathering information. As you have seen, the benefits of a properly utilized CRM process and optimized CRM solution are limitless.

Using a CRM can change the trajectory of your business. Instead of experiencing huge mood swings created by a lack of visibility in the sales pipeline, which can result in layoffs, you now have a tool at your disposal to create a realistic forecast to ensure that your firm has the right resources in place to address future business. Utilization and adoption are key to ensuring that the CRM provides the return on investment you anticipated during the selection process.

CHAPTER 8 KEY SELF-ASSESSMENT

- Are you using your integrated CRM solution as a tool to help your staff, knowing that client relationship management is about process and people, not just a piece of technology?

- Do your employees have access to a unified dataset and understand the story the data is telling?

- Do you empower team members and hold them accountable by using positive reinforcement?

- Do you have a centralized database that saves you time and money, increasing your profitability and efficiencies?

- Do you celebrate adoption and utilization successes at each step of the way along your CRM journey?

- Have you visited our website www.CRMorDie.com to access the additional resources?

9

Protect Your Business Intelligence

"If you are going to achieve excellence in big things,
you develop the habit in little matters.
Excellence is not an exception, it is a prevailing attitude."
— Colin Powell,
Four-Star General

CHAPTER 9 KEY TAKEAWAYS

1. Maintained data is trusted data, which is vital for data-driven decision-making.
2. The cleaner the data, the more accurate the analysis, the better the strategies, and the stronger the business decisions.
3. Data stewardship begins with data policies, standards, and expectations, all of which must be prioritized from the top down.
4. Data hygiene is a practice, not a project; it is developed with small habits that build into data integrity.
5. Employees must be committed to data stewardship, playing their role as data editor, auditor, analyst, consumer, leader, or officer.

As a four-star general, Colin Powell understood excellence. And as the first African American to serve as US Secretary of State, he knew firsthand the power of a prevailing attitude. However, what stands out

"

most about this quote is his focus on habits. His military service started in college and carried him through his 35-year career in the Army, where he developed an appreciation for the habit in little matters. We agree with General Powell and spend this chapter focusing on data habits that will build data stewards in your firm to support a data-driven culture.

Case Study: The Quickest Way to Fail

"I do not use the CRM. I have my own Excel spreadsheet. Let me open it right now to reference all my leads."

That is what a former business development manager told Mycroft, President and Principal in Charge of Safron Architects, in a meeting while they reviewed the open leads. When pressed on why they were not using the CRM, the root issue was distrust in the accuracy of the information.

Mycroft took the time to explain the big picture of how the CRM data was being used to review annual hit rates and other business decisions. He went on to express his expectation that all employees were to enter all data in the integrated CRM solution, and silos spreadsheets were not to be used. He shared his frustration that the dataset he and other principals had been using to make data-driven decisions has been incomplete and inaccurate. He made it clear to all those present at the meeting that the firm's success is directly tied to each person's commitment to enter and maintain data.

"We must ensure data integrity and continue to build user adoption," explained Mycroft. "The quickest way to fail is for distrust to set in, which breeds discontentment and leads to disaster."

Data Stewardship

Referencing back to Chapter 1, you will remember D&B defines data stewardship as the responsibility of ensuring that data policies and standards turn into practice.[27] Company leaders must mandate the creation of data policies and standards and require that they be put in place. They also must hold themselves and the employees accountable to be good data stewards.

As the leader, you set the tone for how others in the firm value data, from its hygiene and quality to its usage and effectiveness. Data stewardship is only successful when cultivated from the top down.

Data Policies, Standards, and Expectations

Data policies should establish definitions, provide a firm foundation of data classifications, identifiers, and categories, explain the necessary change management, and map an efficient and reliable data flow process.

D&B states in an eBook focused on data governance that it "is less about achieving 100% data quality (an arguably unattainable goal, especially when some data must be modeled or synthesized) or fixing every data issue and more about having transparent processes — and ownership that can sustain adequate quality thresholds to support the business. Data governance efforts must also never lose sight of the need to provide business value."[28]

This might sound like a big task — and it is — but it is a vital part of setting things up for success.

Elements to include in your data policies are outlined below, but keep in mind that this is a starting point and not an expansive list.

1. **Mission.** The firm's *why* statement. We spent a good deal of Chapter 1 establishing the business value of a CRM solution and why it is needed now.

2. **Process.** A well-documented map outlining the flow of data, showing points of data collection, usage, and maintenance, with each clearly showing who is responsible for each step and dataset, providing as much transparency as possible.

3. **Change Management.** With the new process come modifications to habits, and those must be as clear as possible, so each employee knows what is being expected of them and why the change is urgent and critical. Daily data management will likely be one of those new habits, but it must be accompanied by accountability.

4. **Definitions.** Key terms used in the process map should all be defined for the specific usage by your firm. For example, a prospect is any potential client in a wide pool of possible clients. A lead, on the other hand, is a client that has been verified as a client with a qualified opportunity. As an example, for a general contractor that specializes in higher education dorms, all universities could be prospects, but only the ones with approved funding to build new dormitories would qualify as leads.

5. **Identifiers.** If you work backward to determine how you want the data reported or displayed on dashboards, the classifications and categories will present themselves. Using the previous example, if they want to know how many beds they put in place year over year, the number of beds for each project needs to be tracked. If they want the cost per square foot for livable space, each project needs cost and livable square footage captured; if they want to know this information for each state or region, then those additional data points need to be gathered.

Data Stewards

With data stewardship defined and communicated to all employees, clear expectations set, and policies written and distributed, it is time for employees to see themselves as data stewards.

Every employee and every department — marketing, BD, operations, leadership, technical staff, even the receptionist — has their own datasets that they are affected by and must understand how to manage well. Each person is responsible for their own data entry and keeping the data current. For data to remain up to date and allow for real-time decision-making, every employee must stay committed to data entry and maintenance. Each person contributes to the success of the company's data culture and should understand their role as a data steward.

Data Roles

As detailed in Chapter 2, one of the key pillars of data stewardship is understanding that **every** single team member has a data role and takes responsibility for their part in the firm's data process and ultimate success or failure. Some may even have multiple roles, depending on the task at hand. These roles can include data editors, auditors, analysts, consumers, leaders, and a data officer.

The data officer directs the ship with the support of the data leaders, analysts, and auditors who take the most proactive role in data stewardship. These are the people who will assist in the creation of data policies and standards and help ensure that they are followed and maintained. These leaders provide the oversight and guidance to stay on track. We encourage you not to let data leaders become bottlenecks by tasking them with all the data entry. Every employee should be responsible for entering the information they possess, interact with, and own. This allows data leaders to stay focused on optimization and leveraging the firm's data assets to their fullest.

Regardless of how many data roles are currently filled, you as the leader need to stress that every employee must understand how important data is to the business's future. Good data allows leaders to make well-informed and data-driven decisions, whereas incomplete or inaccurate data results in poor business decisions and affects *everyone*!

Keep the CRM Open

Every CRM user should be in the system daily or at least several times a week. We always recommend keeping it open on a second monitor for quick access. This allows business developers to quickly enter a new pursuit and project managers to capture client changes with ease. When marketers receive updated information for a proposal, the data should immediately be captured in the CRM, not trapped inside the proposal document. The guiding principle is for all staff members to have access to the same valuable information instead of hiding it in silos.

The frequency of records being edited is a good indicator that employees are dedicated to their roles as data stewards and are advancing the company's data culture. However, editing alone is not enough; auditors must monitor the data and protect data integrity. Remember, the task to populate missing data or correct inaccurate data does not fall to the auditors, but rather, the data editors with the original information. This is an important part of building accountability. The auditors must resist the temptation to populate missing data. The editors need to be correctly entering it into the system. This includes you — the business leader!

Although you have the role of data consumer, you must also enter or have someone enter the valuable information you possess into the CRM system. As a leader, you have unique knowledge that deserves to be captured and protected. In the role of data consumer, you take the knowledge and insights from the analysts and convert that information into competitive advantage to use while making business decisions. This is an active role that requires action. Consumption is not passive!

Todd Park, former Chief Technology Officer of the United States and Technology Advisor for US President Barack Obama, once said, "Data by itself is useless. Data is only useful if you apply it." As leaders and data consumers, you must use it and apply it to your business decisions.[29]

When leadership can request a report with a specific constraint or filter, and it is immediately returned with 90% or more of the data populated and with a 95% or greater accuracy rate, that is a big win. If you are not there yet, lean into the frustration of lacking easily accessible data. Use it to drive the need for a data process, a CRM system, and established data roles.

Data Hygiene

The goal of data stewardship is to protect the business asset of data. To do this requires daily habits. Colin Powell explained how excellence in big things is achieved by developing the necessary habit in little matters. One of those daily habits during his time in the Army was making his bed to military precision. Similarly, one of the best daily habits employees can form is always having the integrated CRM solution open and quickly accessible. This allows for quick data entry, modification, and reference, ensuring usage. Like Powell's daily bed making, daily data entry must happen to maintain data hygiene in the CRM.

As another example, we visit the dentist regularly for dental cleanings and exams. The hygienist cleans off the plaque to get the teeth in top shape before the dentist comes to examine the overall health of the teeth, gums, etc., to provide an assessment of your dental health. They will discuss any areas of concern or things that need to be improved in your daily hygiene routine, like flossing more often.

Data auditors are the hygienists and dentists performing regular exams and looking for areas that need to be cleaned or daily habits that need to be tightened. They cannot brush and floss every employee's teeth for them; that responsibility falls to each employee. But they can monitor the system and provide training and guidance to help the staff with their data hygiene.

Hygiene Is a Practice, Not a Project

If you remember Phillips Lindell Contractors from Chapter 1, their data *why* was all about bonding capacity, and therefore, all pursuits had to be entered into the system at all times. Their data flow process was to have Vaughan, the marketing assistant, enter all basic data to create the record for the pursuit. The BD team member for that market would be notified via a workflow that a new opportunity was in the system. They would log in and populate the go/no-go fields, with a yes/no field about bonding capacity being a required data point. The system calculated a go/no-go score based on the data, and those over a certain threshold were sent to leadership for approval. The system sent an email to the market sector leader recapping the pursuit information with a link to approve or deny the opportunity.

For this process, everyone from the marketing assistant, BD, and market leader had a unique part in the data flow, and all were expected to be good data stewards. The marketing assistant and business developer were data editors, while the market leader was the data leader with oversight responsibilities.

The entire process was audited by Emmalee, the CRM Manager. She ran weekly reports to ensure all the necessary fields were populated and the go/no-go score was properly calculated. If a piece of data was missed, she reached out to the BD lead and requested the information be entered. She also monitored the market leaders to ensure that they were responding in a timely fashion to approve or deny the pursuit requests. If there was a frequent offender not meeting the data expectations or standards, additional training was provided, or measures were taken to hold employees accountable.

When everyone contributes and understands their role in the data process, the company's data asset remains protected and healthy.

> *The cleaner the data, the more accurate the analysis,*
> *the better marketing and business strategies,*
> *and the stronger the business decisions.*

Distrust and Verify

What does it mean to audit data? Essentially, it is the act of looking for missing data, reviewing usage, reducing noise and unused fields, and monitoring operations.

Courtney has been known to tell people to "distrust and verify." At its core, this simply means, do not make any assumptions when it comes to data; know what you are looking at and know what it means.

For example, when you look at a dashboard pipeline, what is being displayed? Is it showing all open pursuits currently in the system, or is it showing all pursuits created that year? What dollar value is being displayed? Is it the full fee, the project cost, the potential revenue, or the factored fee? If there are percentages displayed, are they calculated by dollar volume or quantity of records in that category? Every user needs to understand what they are looking at, but the data auditor needs to know if the dashboard widget is pulling a complete dataset.

Courtney tends to distrust what is being displayed until she can verify with a report that what is being shown is correct. For this reason, we recommend that every dashboard widget have a backup report. For example, if the pipeline widget is pulling all open pursuits in the system by stage and displaying project cost, someone should consistently run a report with those exact constraints to confirm that the information on the dashboard is correct.

We all know bugs get into software, and until someone questions what is being displayed, it tends to be taken at face value. A best practice is to have the data auditor run backup reports monthly to verify that everything is working as expected.

Look for Missing Data

Required fields should also be monitored because there could be ways to bypass requirements or enter a false piece of data to get beyond the requirement. For example, some systems allow you to create records from a mobile app, which may not always honor requirements. Users might enter $1 to get past the fee requirement, which will skew the datasets and result in inaccurate information.

Running regular reports for data the company relies on is important. For example, if marketing sends email campaigns, every contact in the CRM should have an email address. Likewise, if the company sends an annual holiday card or gift, each contact needs an address. When those emails and mailers go out, there will likely be bounces or cards returned, which should all be captured in the CRM. Assignments should also be made to have those contacts updated.

Eliminate Orphaned Contacts

Most companies have thousands, or even tens of thousands, of contacts in their CRM system, and no single person should be responsible for keeping all those records up to date. This is why Courtney stresses the importance of removing orphans from the system. A contact record that is not connected to an internal employee at your firm is considered a lonely orphan. Every contact in the integrated CRM solution needs an owner — an internal person connected to that contact. This is often the person with the relationship or the person who entered the record into the system. If no one knows them, determine if they need to remain in the database. And if they are not needed, make them inactive to reduce clutter.

Eliminating orphans is important for your data integrity and protects your business intelligence. After all, you want to ensure that all business relationships stay connected to your firm. Keeping clients and relationships with your firm is vital. You never want them to walk out the door when an employee leaves or retires.

When Diann, the Director of Business Development at Safron Architects, recently retired, the team ran a report to identify all her contacts. The report was sent to her manager, who divided her contacts in two groups. The contacts that had relationships with existing employees were reassigned, while the remaining contacts went to Diann's replacement. Following best practice suggestions, Safron's employees contacted all of Diann's clients to inform them that Diann had left the firm, to reiterate that their business was important to Safron, and to introduce the new point of contact that will continue to develop the relationship. It is important that every employee understands that **all** contacts are potential clients. You never want valuable relationships to unknowingly fall away. Remember that is how businesses evaporate into irrelevance!

Running reports to look for contacts without owners or email addresses are just two examples of data points that should be regularly monitored. Your data auditors should look for missing information by running maintenance or audit reports in your integrated CRM solution. Visit our website at www.CRMorDie.com for a list of common reports to protect your data integrity and business intelligence.

Excel Is for Data Cleanup

Once a CRM is implemented, all existing Excel spreadsheets need to be banished to promote the utilization of the centralized database. However, Excel is your data cleanup partner!

We know mass data cleanup is part of every system and usually involves Excel .csv files. We also know not everyone is an Excel guru, so we have provided resources to help your data auditors embrace Excel as the best data cleanup companion. Visit our website at www.CRMorDie.com to download the Excel tips.

Data Utilization

Auditors should also review the system quarterly for utilization. If there are features that are not being used, should they be turned off firm-wide or for a specific set of users? Are there values in a value list that are underutilized or not used at all and should be removed? Are there fields that are not populated and should be turned off?

The best way to increase user adoption is to streamline the user interface. Should certain fields be required, or should they be read-only at a certain stage or at a specific dollar threshold?

We recommend that you regularly investigate workflows to improve communication, transparency, and efficiency. Most systems allow email notifications, custom calculations, and set actions, which are great ways to improve and enhance the integrated CRM solution. We share more about this in Chapter 10.

The last piece of data utilization is knowing where and how data is being used in the business. Data silos and misunderstood data can be devastating to a business. The data leaders should be involved in conversations when discussing data utilization, since they are the ones that should understand it the most.

They have the knowledge of data-use trends and best practices and can provide insights into how and where the data is coming from, how it is being displayed, or how it should be used and interrupted.

In addition to data utilization within the business, all data integrations should also be well documented and monitored, more on this in the following chapter.

Data Excellence

We believe data excellence is achieved through an attitude of data stewardship. Fostering an environment in which all employees see themselves as data stewards begins at the top and ends with each person understanding their role in the maintenance process.

It requires equal participation from the data editors, auditors, analysts, leaders, and consumers to achieve data excellence, and it requires a daily commitment from each data steward to keep the CRM platform open, to utilize it often, and to clean it regularly. These habits are often seen as simply and easily ignored.

As Colin Powell said, "If you are going to achieve excellence in big things, you develop the habit in little matters. Excellence is not an exception, it is a prevailing attitude." Creating data policies, standards, and expectations that are reinforced through regular accountability will help solidify these healthy habits.

CHAPTER 9 KEY SELF-ASSESSMENT

- Is your staff responsible for maintaining your data so it can be trusted for your data-driven decision-making?

- Does your firm have a culture of data stewardship?

- Do you have data policies, standards, and expectations prioritized from the top down?

- At your firm, is data hygiene practiced daily to build data integrity, or is it regarded as a one-time project?

- Does every employee understand their data role as an editor, auditor, analyst, consumer, leader, or officer?

- Have you visited our website www.CRMorDie.com to access the additional resources?

10

Enrich Your Vision

"Perfection is achieved, not when there is nothing more to add,
but when there is nothing left to take away."
— Antoine de Saint Exupery,
Writer & Pioneering Aviator

CHAPTER 10 KEY TAKEAWAYS

1. There are countless ways to use automation to reduce data entry, to streamline your process, and optimize your integrated CRM solution.
2. When it comes to integrating systems, simple is better.
3. Always look for ways to reduce duplicate entries.
4. Automation is not just about using what is in the platform; look for other systems to help you automate key functions.

Case Study: Powerful Automations

Circling back to Safron Architects, let's see how they are doing after living in their system for more than a year. Thanks to executive support and a successful rollout, the team found its rhythm and adopted the integrated CRM solution as a vital part of Safron's culture. That said, it was not Greg's style to sit back and rest on his laurels. It was time to enrich the vision he had for the CRM process and system.

During the implementation and onboarding, as they began to adopt the platform, Greg thought about future automations he wanted to do. He had ideas for additional integrations and workflows, plus some innovative ways to use the system. Now seemed like the right time to start putting those ideas into action.

Greg wanted to start with automations because he wholeheartedly believed in his good friend Julie Shaffer's motto, "That which has been typed should never be typed again!" Now that his team had traction in the CRM system, he wanted to find ways to automate and cut out the duplicate effort. He wanted to remove the need for teammates to copy and paste the same information into multiple places in the system or into different systems.

After taking time to prioritize all his ideas, Greg narrowed it down to three automations.

1. Automating how new contacts and companies were added to their email marketing platform.
2. Streamlining the data transferred when an opportunity record was converted to a project.
3. Creating email notifications for leadership when opportunities were created in the system over a certain dollar threshold.

Email Marketing Contacts

During implementation, the CRM team conducted a process-mapping exercise to document the flow of data through the business. One thing that stood out to the team was how difficult and time-consuming it was for marketing to update contacts in the email campaign software. When people subscribed on the website to receive the company newsletter, the information was automatically added to the CRM system.

However, to get that same data over to the email campaign platform, Aydan, the marketing coordinator, had to manually run through a list of all the companies and contacts created in the system in the previous 30 days and export it to Excel. Then she would upload the spreadsheet into the email marketing system and manually review errors and duplicates. This process was inefficient and went against the "that which has been typed should never be typed again" philosophy!

Greg researched the cost of integrating the CRM platform with the email marketing provider, but the fees involved on both sides exceeded his budget. As an interim solution, he decided to do a workaround. He created a workflow in the CRM that triggered every time a new contact was added to the system. An email was sent to marketing with the contact's name, email address, the mailing list category they should be added to, and the name of the user that created the contact. This temporary workaround saved Aydan time and meant the contacts were added more quickly, allowing them to start receiving communication from the company sooner.

Streamline Fields Upon Conversion

Over the last year, several team members commented to Greg how nice it would be to have more fields from the opportunity record automatically added to the project record upon conversion. The current process was for users to go into the CRM system and update the opportunity record once they had received notification that they had won the pursuit. There was a button on the opportunity record labeled 'Convert to Project' that users used to streamline the process of creating the project record.

At first, Greg was hesitant to make changes to this process because of the integration with accounting's financial system that brought key fields into the CRM platform. One of the requested fields to add upon conversion was the dollar amount. During the pursuit phase, the dollar amount of the opportunity was fluid, and Greg was concerned about pushing this to the project once the project was won.

However, after using the CRM platform for a while, Greg could see the advantage in knowing the "starting value" of the project. He decided to incorporate the team's feedback and create a new field in the project record labeled Project Amount at Award. Having the original project amount to compare to the current project amount coming from the accounting system on the same record allowed the team to have some insight into the project financials.

This small change saved Greg from having to run two separate reports from two systems for analysis. The creation of this new field presented an excellent opportunity for further innovation. Greg created a workflow calculation and set it to trigger when a project record was marked as completed. The workflow calculated the difference between the Project Amount at Award and the Final Project Amount. This provided valuable insight to the company leaders and aided in their data-driven decision-making.

Key Opportunity Notifications

After the integrated CRM solution was rolled out, a key issue began to surface at Safron Architects: Leadership was in the dark, unaware of when large pursuits entered the opportunity pipeline.

Greg decided to create a workflow notification to email leadership when an opportunity greater than $50,000 was added to the CRM system. If an opportunity greater than $100,000 was entered, a workflow notification was created to email leadership *and* the company president. This helped leadership stay up to date and aware of the larger projects in the pipeline.

Once the workflow was live, Aydan had an idea that a notification email could help with the go/no-go process. As the marketing coordinator, Aydan was responsible for managing the decision-making process that determined if pursuits were qualified and should be a go or if they should be marked as a no-go. Aydan asked Greg if he could create a workflow that assigned numeric values to some of the opportunity data to calculate an official go/no-go score.

After several trial runs, Greg was able to get the system to generate a go/no-go score based on the information entered when a user created an opportunity record. For example, if the pursuit was less than

$50,000, it received one point. If it was $50,001 to $99,999, it received two points. And if it was $100,000 or more, it received three points. If the user selected 'New' as the client type, that was worth one point, whereas if 'Existing or Previous' was selected, that was worth two points. The pursuits earned five points if the answer to the question asking, "Does Safron Architects have rapport with any of the decision-makers?" was yes. The final step of this innovative idea was to create one more workflow that set the 'Go/No-Go Status' field to a 'Go' or a 'No-Go' based on its total number of points.

This completely removed Aydan's manual work and allowed her to transition from managing the decision-making process to monitoring it instead. She ran a weekly report to make sure every open opportunity had the 'Go/No-Go Status' field populated, ensuring that the workflows were still functioning properly.

As you can see from the examples at Safron Architects, automating key functions can be a great way to ensure that time is not wasted pulling or pushing data from one system to another or typing something that's already been typed. Head over to our website www.CRMorDie.com for a list of automation ideas and suggestions. Automation can also improve communication and help keep team members notified of important events in a timely fashion.

Integrations

Integrations are a great way to take your CRM to the next level. In the Safron Architect case study, Greg decided to integrate the CRM solution with the accounting system. We understand this might not be the best choice for all firms.

The following are a few things to consider when deciding if your CRM system is ready to take the step to use integrations to enrich your CRM vision.

1. State of data in both systems
2. Flow of data between both systems
3. Types of data to flow between systems
4. Type of integration

State of Data

If a firm with a standalone CRM (i.e., no integrations) is interested in integrating with another system, it is important to look at the condition of the existing data in both platforms. Reviewing the information will help you better understand if the integration is a good idea and decide what data should be integrated.

Reviewing the state of data means you look at where the data you want to map over to the other system is located and if that field is well populated. For example, it would be great to have the completion date pushed from the accounting system to the CRM solution. However, that might not be a date that the finance team enters in their system. Mapping a field of data that is never populated is not helpful.

The other thing you need to consider when joining two systems together is the protocol for instances of conflicting data, which is guaranteed to happen. As we previously mentioned, one of the most common diverging fields is the client's company name. For example, accounting might enter a client as *ABC Company, LLC* because that is the legal entity listed on the contract, whereas they list the same company as *ABC Co.* in the CRM system. When these two records are connected, the company names are seen as different, and therefore, a duplicate record is created.

This is when having a process or protocol in place is mandatory. Find out if the integration connector has a system in place to help catch records that are similar or like matches. If not, regularly running a report to help with maintenance will be crucial.

Again, it is critical to create a data flow chart before integrating two systems. (See Chapter 4 for more on process maps.) Keep in mind that a little data cleanup may be necessary before the two systems are integrated to ensure that the key data between the systems align.

Flow of Data

Another factor to consider prior to integration is the data flow between the two systems. First, you must decide if it will be a one-way or two-way integration, which can also be called bi-directional.

In the case of integrating a CRM with a financial system or ERP, it is typical that it would be a single direction. If that is true, it is important to establish which system will be the "source of truth" or the starting point to push data to the other system. For most firms, the source of truth would be the ERP or financial system. What does this mean? The CRM solution will receive information, while the other platform remains unchanged.

If a field in the CRM will be populated or controlled by another system, the best practice is to relabel the field name to indicate this so users have a visual reminder of the flow of data. For example, if the ERP is going to push the dollar amount into the CRM project record and control that field, relabel the field name to have an asterisk at the end or put "ERP" at the end. Or, better yet, put the name of the ERP at the end. This will help CRM users know what to do if they see an incorrect dollar value on a project record. They will know that the integration is populating that data, meaning they need to contact accounting to update the value in the ERP system. Then the correct value will be brought over to the CRM. Otherwise, the user will get frustrated updating the value in the CRM just to have it overwritten and changed back to the incorrect number that night when the integration runs.

To avoid issues, it is important to look at the flow of data and any lists that will be part of the integration to ensure uniformity between both systems.

Types of Data

When it comes to the types of data pulled from one system to another, it should be data that is consistently populated. In many cases, it is best to err on the side of simpler being better.

Many firms make the mistake of trying to integrate every field possible when integrating two systems. Remember, as we discussed in Chapter 2, there is *no* reason to gather data for data's sake. This remains true when it comes to mapping and integrating data between multiple systems. It is best to start with the most important data points first and then circle back and add others as needed.

Prior to integrating, it is important to think about any value lists and/or categorizations that are associated with fields of data you might want to map from one system to the other. Some examples might be a list of office locations, divisions, regions, profit centers, or practice areas. Think about the ways you will want to "slice and dice" your data or how you will want to see it displayed on a dashboard widget. The individual slices of the pie chart must be on a list somewhere in the system in order to group data and report it the way you envision it.

If these category fields are part of the integration, it is *imperative* that they are an **exact** match. Otherwise, the integration will create all the values from the first system and add them to the second one. You then open yourself up to duplicate and inconsistent values causing confusion and messy data.

For example, in the CRM, a division may be listed as *Asia Pacific*, while in the ERP, the value list shows it as *APAC*. When the integration is activated, it will see that *APAC* does not exist in the CRM, so it will create the new value *APAC*. Consequently, users will be unsure which one to use, and records will have one or the other — and might even have both selected. Due to this discrepancy, the affected data will be inconsistent and may lead to mistrust.

*There are countless ways to use automation to
reduce data entry, streamline processes,
and optimize your integrated CRM solution.*

Types of Integrations

Now that we have covered everything involved with the data in an integration, we need to get technical and talk about how integration works.

There are several options for connecting one system to another: API, SQL, a data warehouse, a data lake, the list goes on. There are several factors involved to determine which one is the best for your integration. You need to know what options each platform makes available to its clients. Some SaaS companies do not open their products up to connect to other systems through API or SQL, whereas others might allow it but charge an annual fee.

The details of each type of integration can get complex and are dependent on the capabilities of your firm's IT team. If a firm desires an integration but does not have the in-house resources to build an integration, you will be limited to the integrations the CRM provider has available. It is possible to hire a third-party consultant to create an integration for you. It is also possible that the SaaS company has an option to provide that service to their clients.

If you decide to outsource the work, we recommend asking for one to three references of firms they have completed a similar integration for and are currently active and running. We have seen firms not get what they need because they were told something could happen when, in reality, not all the factors were taken into consideration, and the integration was not possible. Talking with a happy customer confirms what you are looking for is possible.

Depending on the integrated CRM solution you have at your firm, there might be third-party solutions available to you to provide another integration option. When we say "third-party solutions," we are talking about products on the market that are designed to help you connect systems. Two examples we love to use are Microsoft's Power Automate tool and Zapier. Both are online automation tools that push data from one system to another.

In addition to pushing data, there are other functionalities that these programs can perform. You might be looking for your CRM system to perform a specific function, automation, or feature and find that an automation tool could perform that need instead.

For example, your CRM system might allow you to enter the activity you have with your clients, but it does not allow you to set reminders to follow up with clients on your calendar. Using Microsoft Power Automate, you can create calendar invites from the information in your CRM system or automate other tasks that may not be available in your CRM yet.

Connecting two systems through integration can be a great way to reduce duplicate data entry, strengthen both systems, streamline your processes, and bring alignment to two siloed systems. However, it is important to remember that a little data cleanup may be required prior to going live with an integration. You want to confirm parity between systems to reduce errors, duplicates, and the addition of similar values.

Keep the Marriage Interesting

Your CRM journey can feel a lot like the development of a relationship. You may even go through similar phases. Searching for and evaluating all the different CRM platforms to find the best fit for your firm can feel a lot like dating. Once you select "the one" and sign the prenup (contract) with the right CRM system, you are engaged to them and get to spend the next six to eight months implementing and envisioning your future together.

The wedding celebration takes place once the system is implemented, and you start onboarding team members. Trainings are underway with users in the system, the data is populated, and integrations are live.

The first year using the CRM is the honeymoon period, where everything is still somewhat new and users are still excited to get into the system and do what is expected of them. All the decisions made during selection and implementation are fresh in mind, so the commitment level is still high.

The hard work begins after you have had the system for a year and the newness fades. The longer you have the system, the easier it is to take it for granted — to stop doing fun, cool dates — and before you know it, you realize it has been nine months since you last did something special or jazzed up the system. For those reading this who are married, we know you are nodding in understanding. These things do not happen on purpose; they happen over time when our attention is elsewhere.

Taking your CRM to the next level a year or more after implementation is like trying to spice up your marriage. It takes work to keep things interesting. This is where automations, integrations, and auditing your processes can help you spice up your CRM system and enrich the vision you have for your long and fulfilling future of maximizing your relationship with your CRM.

CHAPTER 10 KEY SELF-ASSESSMENT

- Is your firm ready to make improvements to the CRM process and/or the integrated CRM solution?

- Have you reviewed your CRM process mapping for ways to reduce duplicate entries?

- Are you utilizing automations like workflow notifications, emails, or set actions within your integrated CRM solution?

- Have you looked for other systems to help you automate key CRM functions?

- Have you visited our website www.CRMorDie.com to access the additional resources?

11

Time to Lead

"It always seems impossible until it's done."

— **Nelson Mandela, Revolutionary &
President of South Africa**

CHAPTER 11 KEY TAKEAWAYS

1. Be inspired to create a data-driven culture that empowers data stewardship at your firm.
2. Capitalize on your powerful business assets, data, and successful client relationship management.
3. Build the right team of data editor, auditor, analyst, consumer, leader, and, most importantly, data officer.
4. Remember that this is a journey that requires daily commitment. CRM is not a destination or a one-time project with an end date. Data and CRM, when done correctly, are a lifestyle, not a diet.
5. ***The Most Important Takeaway:*** CRM is <u>not</u> about a piece of technology; it is about your people and your process!

It is our sincere hope that this book has empowered you to take ownership of your company's data and set the tone for a company-wide culture of data stewardship.

You now have a clear path forward on your CRM journey. Whether you are at the beginning of the process, are in the middle of evaluating and selecting the right integrated CRM solution, or have a system you are implementing, maintaining, or improving, hopefully you have found what you were looking for at just the right time.

With any luck, you have benefited from our years of experience, the lessons we have learned and shared, and our expertise regarding best practices. Most importantly, we hope we have shared our love for data with you and that you now view data as one of your company's most valuable assets. We believe if you prioritize the data process and appoint the right people to be the data auditor(s) and data leader(s), you will make your client relationship management a success!

High-Level Recap

CRM will only be successful with the proper foundation, which requires firms to first focus internally before seeking external solutions. Remember to follow Albert Einstein's advice and focus 90% of your effort on planning and 10% on the end result. This involves a well-defined and documented process that is supported from the top-down.

Take the time to gain a firm-wide understanding of what an integrated CRM solution will fix or resolve for the business. Know why the company needs a CRM now and how it will happen. Leadership must lead by example and be transparent in sharing how data drives the business and how it is being used to drive decision-making. Leadership buy-in is critical and must be in place for the CRM process and technology tool to be successful. Lastly, remember that employees are most successful when expectations are well-defined and accountability is practiced.

Data is an asset and should be treated as the valuable company resource it is, building the foundation of the firm's leadership-led, data-driven culture. Have a plan and know what you are going to do with data before you collect it. Use data to increase profitability, effectiveness, and efficiency. Be a data champion, viewing data as a lifestyle you committed to, and work hard to keep. Take action to create a culture of data stewardship, establish data roles, and invest in a data leader. Above all, we challenge you to dream of your data utopia and then bring it to life.

Prioritizing data is important and goes hand in hand with the benefits of CRM. It is a critical tool in managing the relationships that can help firms win more work. When done right, CRM increases profitability, creates heightened efficiency, grows production, centralizes data, and can even improve morale due to the improved transparency and accountability.

In order to reap these rewards, a company's internal processes must be documented using our five steps: map, identify, review, improve, monitor. It is also best to take the time to flip the perspective and map your CX. In addition to process, a change management strategy must be in place prior to selecting and implementing a CRM solution.

> *CRM is <u>not</u> about a piece of technology.*
> *It is about your people and your process!*

Prior to searching for integrated CRM solutions, take the time to review your answers to all of the questions we outlined in Chapters 4 through 6. Interview staff and stay in control of the selection process. You want to drive, not be driven! Spend the necessary resources and effort to clean your data and break down silos prior to implementation, as the entire process works better when you do. Once you do get to implementation, remember that training is essential, and stay focused on the core aspects of the CRM.

Remember, a CRM is a tool to help humans and not replace them. Ultimately, having a CRM database will save money and increase efficiency. As your team onboards with the new platform, remember to use positive reinforcement with adoption milestones.

Maintenance and hygiene are not glamourous, but they are necessary. Data that is cared for is trusted data, which is vital for data-driven decision-making. This is what happens with a culture of data stewardship, which begins with data policies, standards, and expectations prioritized from the top down. When employees take their role as data stewards seriously, data hygiene is seen as an important practice, not a project. Everyone understands that data integrity is developed with small daily habits that lead to excellence. As a firm continues to work within a CRM, it is important to look for ways to reduce duplicate entries and use automation within the CRM and third-party solutions.

Next Steps

Pass this book on! If you are a firm leader, give this book to your fellow partners or principals. Encourage them to join you as you create a data-driven culture of data stewardship focused on CRM. Provide this book to your data auditors and data leaders, whether that is a CRM manager, chief data officer, both, or someone in between. Ensure that data policies, standards, and expectations are created and put in place, but do not forget to establish accountability — including with you.

If you are not in a leadership position, encourage your leader to read this book to understand their role in the firm's successful management of client relationships. In the meantime, observe upper management to figure out what data they are missing and what information they need or could use to be better educated in making business decisions. Listen for an opportunity to raise this topic and seize the moment!

Reread the chapter(s) that align with where you are in your CRM journey — preparation, evaluation, implementation, utilization, maintenance, or improvement. Once you know where you currently are and where you need to go, take action to move forward. Be the data leader and set the example for stewardship.

Case Study: An Operations Transformation

Most professional services firms in the AEC industry submit quality proposals and then wait for prospects to respond. CDP Construction goes a step further, but that has not always been the case. Five years ago, the firm committed to integrating internal systems and processes, which led to company-wide improvements.

Now, after submitting a strategic proposal, CDP's marketing team refers to real-time CRM data and updates the firm's website. They highlight relevant projects that match the market for their latest proposal. If they are seeking construction work for a school, for example, they will feature signature school projects on their homepage. They also may create relevant social media posts. When prospects conduct online research, CDP's key projects will be readily available for review.

CKearney Consulting (CKC) customized CDP's use of their cloud-based client relationship management software specially designed and developed for the AEC industry. With one click, CDP's marketing team can review its calendar for a summary of proposal and bid due dates, as well as upcoming marketing activities, such as groundbreaking events. This transparency and centralized data allow them to implement strategic measures quickly.

CDP Executive Vice President of Marketing and Communications Deon Smith said they were still learning how to maximize this software for their needs. The marketing team wants to continue improving efficiencies between its offices in Dallas, Texas, and Chattanooga, Tennessee. "Now we have more data accuracy," he said. "We can trust the information that is in our CRM because there is more transparency and accountability. It is a single source of truth."

Before working with CKC, the company's bid calendar required manual input by one person. As a result, data was sometimes incomplete or unavailable. After working with CKC, the construction firm implemented data entry requirements and, through a seamless automated process, the calendar is continually updated. This company saves hours of preparation time every week. Besides the marketing team, several other departments rely on the CRM. BD, accounting, and operations all use the improved dashboards to keep their finger on the pulse of their business pipeline and opportunities.

Overcoming Disjointed Data

A few years ago, CDP had disjointed data in multiple systems. The company did not have a central location for critical dates and data. They used one CRM system for BD activities and a different CRM, plus other platforms to house marketing and project data. Eventually, CDP's management agreed that the multiple systems and complex processes no longer met their needs. Management decided the integrated CRM solution would be the single source of truth. There was an expiring contract for one of CDP's alternate systems, which put an urgent deadline on the project. To successfully implement this change in a short time frame, CDP turned to CKearney Consulting for help.

Deon met Courtney a few years earlier while attending a CKC training session. There, she emphasized her "that which has been typed should never be typed again" policy.

That rule resonated with Deon. He realized CDP was entering data multiple times in different locations. He knew their system needed an updated approach. During the transition process, CKC provided a bridge between CDP and the SaaS provider.

"Courtney can ask the right questions and talk tech," Deon said. For anyone considering implementing an AEC CRM, Deon said their first action should be to budget for the software, and their second move should be to call CKC for customized solutions.

Call to Action

You are now equipped to take on the challenge to successfully manage your client relationships! Decide right now that your firm is going to create a culture of data stewardship and roll out data roles for each employee with specific KPIs tied to their annual reviews for accountability.

This is the time to implement an integrated CRM solution or overhaul and utilize the CRM system you have been neglecting or underutilizing. Demand that your firm stop neglecting the valuable asset and renewable resource of data. It is time to lead!

Finally, review all the self-assessments at the end of each chapter to ensure that you are in the best position to be the CRM champion and the leader your firm needs.

Connect With Us

We sincerely hope this book has empowered you, the business leader, to embrace the fact that the fate of your company relies on you accepting two core principles: Data is everything, and the process around managing your client relationships must be prioritized, maintained, and maximized.

Leaders who understand that data is everything will make data-driven decisions and create a culture that encourages every employee to make their decisions based on data. For that to be possible, there must be an accessible system that centralizes the data, and your integrated CRM solution is the perfect place to capture all that vital information.

Regardless of where you currently find yourself on your CRM journey, we are optimistic that this book has inspired you to jump-start or optimize your client relationship management process and tools. Hopefully, we have proven that a business with a well-defined CRM process and a properly implemented and supported CRM system is able to thrive on data and keep the business moving forward, ensuring that it will not perish!

We would love to hear from you. Please reach out to share where you are in your CRM journey, what value you gained from this book, and how you are using your CRM process, data, and system to thrive.

Connect with us through our website or social media, or book us to come speak at an industry or business event. We are also available to provide our expertise through the consulting services provided by CKearney Consulting.

We are here to help you with all your data and CRM needs, and we look forward to hearing from you soon!

FINAL SELF-ASSESSMENT

- Have you visited our website www.CRMorDie.com to access the additional resources?

- Have you connected with Courtney and Chaz on social media, booked them for an event, or retained the consulting services of CKC?

- Are you inspired to create a data-driven culture that empowers data stewardship?

- Are you ready to capitalize on the power of data and successful client relationship management?

- Are you building the right team of data editors, auditors, analysts, consumers, and leaders?

- If you do not already have a data officer, have you identified someone to serve in this role or started the process of creating the position?

- Are you excited about the CRM journey that lies ahead and committed to seeing it as a lifestyle and not a one-time project?

- Most importantly, are you dedicated to leading a company that understands that CRM is not about a piece of technology, but instead about process and people?

Key Terms

Account-based marketing (ABM): A business strategy that concentrates marketing resources on a set of target accounts or clients, also known as the "rifle" approach, as opposed to the "shotgun" approach.

Application programming interface (API): A connection between computers or between computer programs — often a software interface that offers a service to other pieces of software.

Business intelligence: The strategies and technologies used by enterprises for the data analysis of business information.

Business-to-business (B2B): Companies that do business with other companies, usually selling professional services instead of selling products to consumers.

Business-to-consumer (B2C): Companies selling goods or services to individuals to consume.

Client: A person or business with whom a financial transaction for services has been completed.

Client experience (CX): Strategy of viewing and documenting the journey a client takes when engaging the business.

Client relationship management (CRM): The act of managing client relationships, which involves all employees in a firm.

Dashboard: A collection of widgets, providing an overview of the data you care about most, allowing you to quickly check the health of your company.

Data analyst: A person who takes data and turns it into information and knowledge to extract insights.

Data auditor: A person responsible for monitoring information, systems, and processes to ensure functionality and efficiency.

Data consumer: A person who takes the knowledge and insights generated by data analysts and turns that information into competitive advantage, and uses it to make data-driven decisions.

Data editor: A person responsible for entering data on a consistent and timely basis.

Data leader: A person whose primary focus is creating data policies, standards, and processes, and who also oversees the information systems and data flow between integrated platforms.

Data stewardship: A business practice that holds employees responsible for following and maintaining the data policies, standards, and processes in place.

Data storytelling: A method of communicating data analytics, trends, and insights in the form of a narrative or story. It is a proactive way for everyone to receive a unified data message instead of relying on each employee to find answers and form conclusions of their own.

Go live/launch date: The act of implementing a process or platform or unveiling a new product at a specific and organized time.

Go/no-go process: A structured and strategic framework for making decisions to accept or reject something based on a defined set of criteria.

Hit rate: The percentage, ratio, or number of projects a company wins, usually on an annual basis. This can also be reflected in the number, percentage, or ratio of proposals a company submits that are accepted in a specific timeframe.

Integrated CRM solution: A firm-wide system that is integrated into the flow of data to capture company, contact, pursuit, and project information to support managing client relationships, internal processes, and asset management.

Key performance indicator (KPI): A performance objective tailored to an individual or group that is actionable and quantifiable, and is a goal the individual or group will be held accountable for completing.

Lead: A client who has been verified as having a qualified opportunity.

Production environment: The environment where a user can see, experience, and interact with data in a technological platform, as opposed to the staging environment.

Prospect: Any potential client in the wide pool of possible clients.

Quality assurance/quality control (QA/QC): A combination of quality assurance (the process or set of processes used to measure and ensure the quality of something) and quality control (the process of ensuring that something meets policy standards and expectations).

Request for proposal (RFP): A formal document from a company soliciting a statement of qualification for a separate organization bidding on work.

Software as a service (SaaS): Software hosted by a third-party provider and delivered to customers over the internet as a service, such as TurboTax.

Staging environment: The replica of a production environment where software is tested and features are modified before they are live on a visible site that is available to end-users.

Structured query language (SQL): A domain-specific language programmed and designed for managing structured data (date incorporating relations among entities and variables).

Thought leadership: The expression of ideas that demonstrate expertise in a particular field, area, or topic.

User acceptance testing (UAT): The final phase of software testing that verifies whether a product or software is fit for the purpose it was built for and fulfills end-user requirements.

User interface (UI): A space where interactions between humans and machines occur.

Widget: In the context of a CRM system, a mini report displaying data in a variety of presentation styles, including simple numeric metrics, tables, charts, and graphs.

Acknowledgments

We want to thank our loving families who show us endless support and encouragement.

A big thanks to our CKearney Consulting family for the unending support and feedback as we worked on this book: Carisa Blackmon, Courtney Vance, Erica Curtis, Heather Stacy, Kim Sheldon, Rebecca Joslin, and Valerie Delafosse.

We appreciate Nancy Usrey's beautiful contribution to our work and the time she dedicated to writing such a strong foreword.

This book wouldn't be what it is without our amazing editing team. We are grateful to Jessica Hesse for being the first set of eyes on our words. Her insights and edits strengthened the book's structure and concepts.

Thank you to our editorial project management team, led by Karen Rowe, for providing excellent advice throughout this process — first through her book *Behind the Cover*, which kicked off our journey, followed by private coaching calls, accountability, and editorial support.

This book would not have been possible without the continued support of our partners, Brendan Kearney and Greg Ross-Munro, and our children: Emmalee Kearney, Aydan Kearney, and Mycroft Ross-Munro. We love each of you more than words can express!

Supplemental Resources

Organizational Charts

The case studies and stories we shared in this book involved several key players within the firm. We find that visuals help keep everyone's roles clear, so we have included the organizational charts.

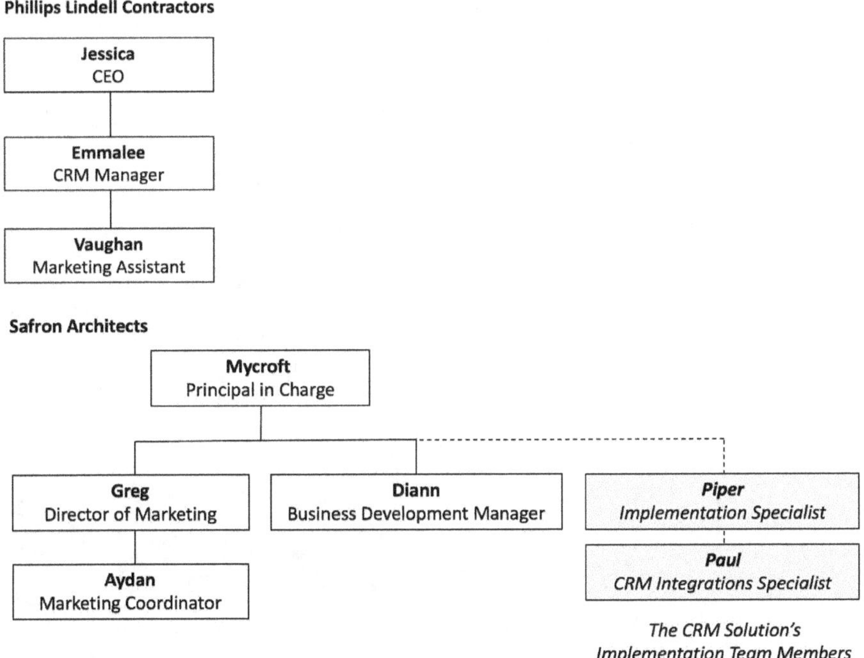

The CRM Solution's
Implementation Team Members

Brueggemann Civil Engineering

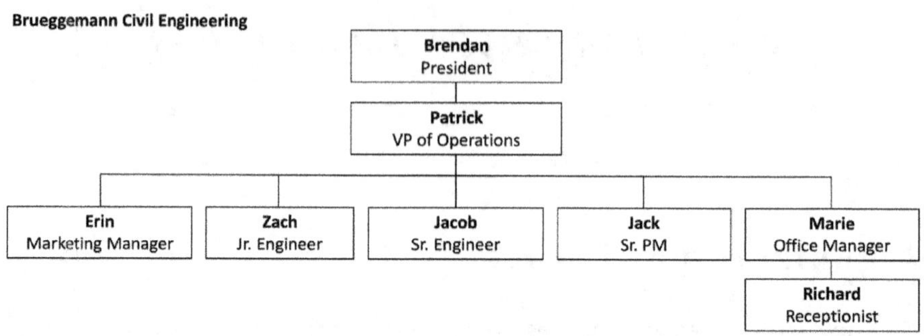

Citations

Chapter 1

[1] Butcher, Scott D. "Marketing 2022." SMPS Publishes Report on Current and Anticipated A/E/C Marketing Practices. The Society for Marketing Professional Services (SMPS), November 18, 2019. https://www.smps.org/smps-publishes-report-on-current-and-anticipated-a-e-c-marketing-practices.

[2] Butcher, Scott D. The CRM Imperative for AEC Firms. Engineering News-Record, January 20, 2021. https://www.enr.com/blogs/22-marketropolis/post/51006-the-crm-imperative-for-aec-firms.

[3] Cramer, Jonathan James. "Why You Need a Data Steward and Best Practices to Do It Right." 6 Key Responsibilities of the Invaluable Data Steward. Dun & Bradstreet, March 5, 2019. https://www.dnb.com/perspectives/master-data/6-key-responsibilities-of-data-stewards.html.

[4] Snyder, Jay, Alyssa Menard, and Natalie Spare. "Big Data = Big Questions for the Engineering and Construction Industry." Big Data Report. FMI, November 2018. https://fmicorp.com/wp-content/uploads/2018/11/FMI_BigDataReport.pdf.

[5] Laforest, Toby. Construction Data Forecast for 2021. Engineering News-Record, March 18, 2021. https://tinyurl.com/xwyfck4e.

[6] Bridle, James. Opinion: Data isn't the new oil — it's the new nuclear power. Ideas.Ted.Com, July 17, 2018. https://ideas.ted.com/opinion-data-isnt-the-new-oil-its-the-new-nuclear-power.

[7] Mavuduru, Amol. Is Data Really the New Oil in the 21st Century? Towards Data Science, December 11, 2020. https://towardsdatascience.com/is-data-really-the-new-oil-in-the-21st-century-17d014811b88.

[8] "Survey Reveals One in Five Businesses Loses Revenue and Customers Due to Incomplete Data." Dun & Bradstreet Releases New Report on Data Management. Dun & Bradstreet, June 24, 2019. https://www.dnb.com/perspectives/newsroom/dun-bradstreet-data-management-report-release.html.

Chapter 2

[9] Snyder, Jay, Alyssa Menard, and Natalie Spare. "Big Data = Big Questions for the Engineering and Construction Industry." Big Data Report. FMI, No-

vember 2018. https://fmicorp.com/wp-content/uploads/2018/11/FMI_Big-DataReport.pdf.

[10] Laforest, Toby. Construction Data Forecast for 2021. Engineering News-Record, March 18, 2021. https://tinyurl.com/xwyfck4e.

[11] Fiorina, Carly. "Information: the currency of the digital age." HP Carly Fiorina Speech: Information: the currency of the digital age. HP, December 6, 2004. http://www.hp.com/hpinfo/execteam/speeches/fiorina/04open-world.html.

[12] Butcher, Scott D. "Marketing 2022." SMPS Publishes Report on Current and Anticipated A/E/C Marketing Practices. The Society for Marketing Professional Services (SMPS), November 18, 2019. https://www.smps.org/smps-publishes-report-on-current-and-anticipated-a-e-c-marketing-practices.

[13] Butcher, Scott D. The CRM Imperative for AEC Firms. Engineering News-Record, January 20, 2021. https://www.enr.com/blogs/22-marketropolis/post/51006-the-crm-imperative-for-aec-firms.

[14] Kruse, Kevin. The 80/20 Rule And How It Can Change Your Life. Forbes Magazine, March 7, 2016. https://www.forbes.com/sites/kevinkruse/2016/03/07/80-20-rule/?sh=6f35e8f43814.

[15] "A/E/C Business Development Bible." E-Book: A/E/C Business Development Bible. PSMJ Resources, Inc., 2015. https://go.psmj.com/ebook-business-development-bible.

[16] Pettey, Christy, and Rob van der Meulen. Gartner Survey Finds Chief Data Officers Are Delivering Business Impact and Enabling Digital Transformation. Gartner, Inc., December 6, 2017. https://www.gartner.com/en/newsroom/press-releases/2017-12-06-gartner-survey-finds-chief-data-officers-are-delivering-business-impact-and-enabling-digital-transformation.

[17] Wiles, Jackie. Do You Need a Chief Data Officer? Gartner, Inc., May 18, 2021. https://www.gartner.com/smarterwithgartner/do-you-need-a-chief-data-officer.

[18] Goasduff, Laurence. Gartner Predicts by 2023, 50% of Chief Digital Officers in Organizations Without a Chief Data Officer (CDO) Should Become the De Facto CDO to Ensure Success. Gartner, Inc., January 19, 2021. https://www.gartner.com/en/newsroom/press-releases/2021-01-19-gartner-predicts-that-50-percent-of-chief-digital-officers-to-become-the-de-facto-cdo-to-succeed.

Chapter 4

[19] "Survey Reveals One in Five Businesses Loses Revenue and Customers Due to Incomplete Data." Dun & Bradstreet Releases New Report on Data Management. Dun & Bradstreet, June 24, 2019. https://www.dnb.com/perspectives/newsroom/dun-bradstreet-data-management-report-release.html.

Chapter 5

20 Butcher, Scott D. "Marketing 2022." SMPS Publishes Report on Current and Anticipated A/E/C Marketing Practices. The Society for Marketing Professional Services (SMPS), November 18, 2019. https://www.smps.org/smps-publishes-report-on-current-and-anticipated-a-e-c-marketing-practices.

21 Kotter, Dr. John. The 8-step Process for Leading Change. Kotter, 2018. https://www.kotterinc.com/8-steps-process-for-leading-change.

22 Brown, Marcel. 1000 Songs in Your Pocket. This Day in Tech History, October 23, 2001. https://thisdayintechhistory.com/10/23/1000-songs-in-your-pocket.

Chapter 6

23 Abrams, Stacey. 3 questions to ask yourself about everything you do. TEDWomen, November 2018. https://www.ted.com/talks/stacey_abrams_3_questions_to_ask_yourself_about_everything_you_do?language=en.

24 Butcher, Scott D. "Marketing 2022." SMPS Publishes Report on Current and Anticipated A/E/C Marketing Practices. The Society for Marketing Professional Services (SMPS), November 18, 2019. https://www.smps.org/smps-publishes-report-on-current-and-anticipated-a-e-c-marketing-practices.

25 "The Annual ConTech Report." Get access to the 2020 construction technology report. JBKnowledge. Accessed November 5, 2021. https://jbknowledge.com/2020-construction-technology-report-survey.

Chapter 8

26 Guthridge, Liz. Recently Succeed At Something? Celebrating Is Good For Your Brain. Forbes Magazine, June 24, 2019. https://www.forbes.com/sites/forbescoachescouncil/2019/06/24/recently-succeed-at-something-celebrating-is-good-for-your-brain/?sh=c7cc71a3d916.

Chapter 9

27 Cramer, Jonathan James. "Why You Need a Data Steward and Best Practices to Do It Right." 6 Key Responsibilities of the Invaluable Data Steward. Dun & Bradstreet, March 5, 2019. https://www.dnb.com/perspectives/master-data/6-key-responsibilities-of-data-stewards.html.

28 Shannon, Kevin. Data Governance Is Mission Critical for Dun & Bradstreet. Dun & Bradstreet, December 2018. https://tinyurl.com/mh4xs3fa.

29 Greenebarrett. Data by itself is useless. Barrett and Greene, June 9, 2017. https://www.greenebarrett.com/post/data-by-itself-is-useless.

www.ingramcontent.com/pod-product-compliance
Lightning Source LLC
Chambersburg PA
CBHW071319150726
47997CB00002B/529

9 798985 141603